THE AMERICAN ANOMALY

THE AMERICAN ANOMALY

U.S. Politics and Government in Comparative Perspective

Raymond A. Smith

Routledge
Taylor & Francis Group
New York   London

Routledge
Taylor & Francis Group
270 Madison Avenue
New York, NY 10016

Routledge
Taylor & Francis Group
2 Park Square
Milton Park, Abingdon
Oxon OX14 4RN

© 2008 by Raymond A. Smith
Routledge is an imprint of Taylor & Francis Group, an Informa business

Printed in the United States of America on acid-free paper
10 9 8 7 6 5 4 3 2 1

International Standard Book Number-13: 978-0-415-95746-5 (Softcover) 978-0-415-95745-8 (Hardcover)

Library of Congress Cataloging-in-Publication Data

Smith, Raymond A., 1967-
  The American anomaly : U.S. politics and government in comparative perspective /
Raymond A. Smith.
    p. cm.
  Includes bibliographical references and index.
  ISBN 978-0-415-95745-8 (hbk : alk. paper) -- ISBN 978-0-415-95746-5 (pbk : alk.
paper)
    1. United States--Politics and government--2001- 2. Comparative government. I.
Title.

JK275.S56 2007
320.473--dc22   2007016113

Visit the Taylor & Francis Web site at
http://www.taylorandfrancis.com

and the Routledge Web site at
http://www.routledge.com

Contents

Preface

This book comes directly out of discussion and interaction with my students over the past five years. Over that time, I have had the opportunity to teach introductory American politics courses in a wide variety of settings, including in small, almost seminar-style courses in an adult BA program, in a medium-sized lecture format at a public college, and in large lecture hall settings at a major university. Regardless of the school or the format of the class, I consistently found that students are eager for information about the politics and governments of other countries, particularly for the insights about the United States that can be provided by the comparative approach.

Thus was born the idea for *The American Anomaly: U.S. Politics and Government in Comparative Perspective*. This brief volume does not aim to review all aspects of the U.S. political system—that is the task of a conventional introductory American politics textbook. Nor does it seek to systematically cover all of the major variations found in the government and politics of the countries of the world—that is the job of a comparative politics textbook. Rather, this volume has a different goal: to shed new light on key institutions, processes, and other dimensions of the U.S. political system by examining how these are organized and practiced differently in other countries of the world. The hope is that by examining the full menu of political processes and governmental institutions cross-nationally, students might be able to achieve greater insight into the impact of such differences for the nature and quality of democractic representation and governance in the United States.

Studying how different countries choose to organize their politics is not only a valuable academic endeavor. It is also a valuable civic undertaking, suggesting how an already robust democracy in the United States can learn from the experience of other political systems, and also identifying features of the U.S. system that might be helpful in other countries. Over the course of this book, a number of striking patterns about the anomalous character of U.S. politics will emerge, including that:

- Among the twenty-two countries that have been independent and steadily democratic since 1950, only one other (Costa Rica) employs a strict separation-of-powers political system with a powerful president, institutionally insulated from the legislature, who serves as both head of state and head of government.
- Among these twenty-two countries, most have a lower house of parliament with far more power than the upper house, unlike the United States in which both houses have equal law-making authority. Also, in only a handful of others (notably Britain and Canada) are the members of the lower house of the legislature elected through a simple-majority electoral system.
- Of the nearly two dozen countries in the Western hemisphere with a separation of powers system, every one except the United States has experienced a collapse of democracy into dictatorship since World War II.
- While judiciaries around the world are growing in significance, virtually none has the sweeping power of the U.S. federal courts to make authoritative rulings about constitutional interpretation.
- Many countries have multiparty systems in which five, six, or even a dozen or more parties routinely play a meaningful role in politics; the stable, long-term two-party system found in the United States is a true rarity.
- At first glance, U.S. public opinion appears to be in the middle of the pack among nations of the world, but on closer

inspection it becomes clear that American attitudes are more liberal than almost all developing countries but more conservative than almost all developed countries.

Despite these anomalies, I have found that many American students reflexively assume that the U.S. political system must somehow be the best system in the world, and that other countries are eager to emulate it. Some felt that democracy itself required that politics and government be organized as it is in the United States. A few thought that it might be somehow unpatriotic or antidemocratic to critically assess the strengths and weaknesses of politics in the United States by comparing it with other countries. And a smaller, but consistent, number were highly critical of the United States, arguing that other countries would be better off avoiding the institutions and processes of the American political system.

This volume holds that every political system maximizes some values at the expense of others. For example, oppressive dictatorships can provide a great deal of stability, but few people would choose to live in such a system because of the freedom, equality, responsiveness, flexibility, and other values that would be compromised. Even within the family of democracies, different approaches to political institutions and processes can emphasize some values over others. To highlight these comparisons, extended case studies are presented in each chapter drawing upon all of the major regions of the world, including Western Europe, Eastern Europe, the Middle East, Sub-Saharan Africa, Southeast Asia, East Asia, Latin America, North America, and Oceania. While individual examples are drawn from dozens of political systems, a special emphasis is paid to the twenty-two countries that have been independent and steadily democratic since 1950, a group consisting largely of Western European parliamentary democracies. (The political systems of these twenty-two countries are systematically compared in Table 1 following this preface.) Given their strong historical and cultural linkages to the United States, a particular focus is placed on the English-speaking nations of the British Commonwealth, with every chapter specifically structured to include some discussion of politics or government in both Canada and Great Britain.

A Note to Instructors

The American Anomaly is designed primarily to be used as a supplemental textbook in introductory American politics courses for those professors who wish to employ a comparative perspective that goes beyond the brief boxed features about other countries that are so common in textbooks. To this end, it is intentionally organized to parallel the usual chapter headings found in the core introductory American politics textbooks, and it is assumed that students have, or at least have access to, such textbooks. However, the book can also be used profitably in other courses, most notably introductory comparative politics classes. Frequently, the textbooks for such comparative politics provide single-chapter coverage of the politics and governments of various countries, but often the United States is—perplexingly—*not* included in such texts. (For an overview of the comparative content of *The American Anomaly*, see Table 2.)

The American Anomaly may be of particular value to the increasing number of students who were raised or educated outside the United States, who may find this volume helpful in translating their understanding of politics from their own country to the American context. It can also be a useful introduction for American students who are beginning to study the politics of other countries, particularly those with parliamentary governments.

To keep this volume relatively brief and readily accessible to a wide range of students, many topics have not been included. For instance, the study of how modern mass media frame political issues or how public opinion surveys achieve random samples is important, but these topics are not discussed in this volume because the comparative approach would not particularly shed much light on them. Likewise, topics that might be extremely important in the study of some other countries, such as details of how parliamentary coalitions are formed in Western Europe or how the military plays a political role in Central Africa, do not have much relevance to the study of U.S. politics and, thus, are also excluded from this volume.

Similarly, *The American Anomaly* is informed by the long and rich tradition of studies on the cultural and historical roots of American Exceptionalism. However, it does not directly engage that literature, partly in order to offer a fresh perspective and partly to provide an institutionally oriented approach that will make this volume a good fit for use alongside most introductory American politics textbooks. Because this book will, ideally, be just the starting point of the comparative study of the U.S. political system for many students, a brief bibliographic essay on American exceptionalism is provided at the end of the book.

Finally, discussion of U.S. public policy, including civil liberties and civil rights, has been woven throughout the book rather than broken off into separate chapters. At various points, readers will find consideration of how anomalous features of the American political system have affected public policy in areas as diverse as freedom of expression, freedom of religion, the right to bear arms, due process guarantees, social welfare spending, taxation policies, education, disaster relief, racial integration, war powers, foreign policy, and immigration.

As the instructor wishes, individual chapters of this book may be assigned when various topics are discussed throughout the semester. Given the brevity of this volume, it can also be assigned as a whole at the outset of the semester, or each of the four parts of the book may be assigned together at appropriate points in the course. The parts may be read in any order, although it is recommended that Part I be read first, particularly Chapter 4 which introduces the parliamentary system of government. It is also beneficial for Chapters 8 and 9 to be read sequentially. Each chapter includes suggestions for further reading, one exercise for Web-based exploration, and a chapter question, which can be used as the basis for a written assignment and/or a classroom discussion.

Acknowledgments

I would like to thank the four students at Columbia University who worked as research assistants on this project: Victoria Kwan, Kwame Spearman, Howard Kline, and Alison Cordova. I am also grateful for the help and encouragement offered by friends and colleagues including Kim Johnson, Shareen Hertel, Laura Nathanson, Martin Good, Susan Roberts, and Vickie and Bernie Candon. In addition, I would like to acknowledge the support of the chairs or heads of the political science departments at Columbia University, Barnard College, New York University, and Hunter College in which I have taught, particularly Robert Shapiro, Kenneth Sherrill, Richard Pious, Kimberley Marten, Shinasi Rama, and Veena Thedani. Most of all, I would like to thank the many students, now numbering over two thousand, who have studied American politics and government with me over the past six years. I have learned an enormous amount from their ideas and questions, their insights and their enthusiasm, and I dedicate this book to them.

Table 1 Comparison of twenty-two established democracies

COUNTRY	YEAR OF CURRENT CONSTITUTION	UNITARY OR FEDERAL?	SEPARATION OF POWERS?	HEAD OF STATE	HEAD OF GOVERNMENT	STRUCTURE OF LEGISLATURE	JUDICIAL REVIEW?	ELECTORAL SYSTEM	PARTY SYSTEM
United States	1789	Federal, with fifty states	Yes	President elected by the Electoral College, which is allocated according to popular vote		Symmetric bicameralism, both houses popularly elected	Supreme Court and other federal courts have judicial review	Single member plurality	Two-party
Australia	1901	Federal system with six states and two territories	Some; upper house and High Court can check the executive	Ceremonial governor-general, appointed by prime minister, represents British monarch	Prime minister elected by lower house of parliament	Symmetric bicameral parliament; both houses popularly elected	High Court has judicial review	Single member plurality in lower house; Proportional representation in Senate	Two-party plus
Austria	1920; restored in 1945 after World War II	Federal system with nine states	No	Popularly elected ceremonial president	Chancellor elected by lower house of parliament	Asymmetric bicameral parliament; both houses popularly elected	Constitutional court has limited judicial review	Proportional representation	Multi-party
Belgium	1831	Federal system with three regions and three language communities	No	Hereditary ceremonial monarch	Prime minister elected by lower house of parliament	Asymmetric bicameral parliament; both houses popularly elected (some seats in upper house are appointed)	High Council for Justice has limited judicial review	Proportional representation	Multi-party

Table 1 Comparison of twenty-two established democracies (continued)

COUNTRY	YEAR OF CURRENT CONSTITUTION	UNITARY OR FEDERAL?	SEPARATION OF POWERS?	HEAD OF STATE	HEAD OF GOVERNMENT	STRUCTURE OF LEGISLATURE	JUDICIAL REVIEW?	ELECTORAL SYSTEM	PARTY SYSTEM
Canada	1867; Charter of Rights and Freedoms added in 1982	Federal; ten provinces and three territories	No	Ceremonial governor-general, appointed by prime minister, represents British monarch	Prime minister elected by lower house of parliament	Asymmetric bicameral parliament; lower house popularly elected, upper house appointed	Supreme Court has judicial review but can be over-ridden	Single-member plurality	Two-party plus
Costa Rica	1949	Unitary	Yes	Popularly elected president		Unicameral legislative assembly	Supreme Court of Justice has significant judicial review	Proportional representation for legislature; single-member plurality for president	Two-party plus
Denmark	1953	Unitary, but with home rule for two overseas territories	No	Hereditary ceremonial monarch	Prime minister elected by lower house of parliament	Unicameral parliament, popularly elected	Supreme Court does not have judicial review	Multimember proportional representation	Multi-party
Finland	1919	Unitary	Some; president and parliament can check each other	Popularly elected president with some significant powers	Prime Minister elected by lower house of parliament	Unicameral parliament, popularly elected	Supreme Court does not have judicial review	Multimember proportional representation	Multi-party

France	1958	Unitary	Only when president and parliamentary majority are of different parties	Popularly elected president with very significant powers	Prime minister appointed by president, confirmed by lower house of parliament	Asymmetric bicameral parliament; lower house popularly elected, upper house indirectly elected from regions	Court of Cassation does not have judicial review; there is a Constitutional Court within the executive	Multimember proportional representation for lower house of parliament; runoff elections for president	Multi-party
Germany	1949	Federal; sixteen Länder	Some; upper house can block laws on issues related to the Länder	Ceremonial president elected by parliament and Länder legislatures	Chancellor elected by lower house of parliament	Limited asymmetric bicameralism; popularly elected lower house, upper house appointed by Länder	Constitutional Court has judicial review	Mixed single-member plurality and proportional representation	Multi-party
Great Britain	No written constitution	Unitary, with devolved powers to Northern Ireland, Scotland, Wales	No	Hereditary ceremonial monarch	Prime minister elected by lower house of parliament	Strongly asymmetric bicameralism; popularly elected lower house, mostly appointed upper house	Law lords do not have judicial review	Single-member plurality	Two-party plus

Table 1 Comparison of twenty-two established democracies (continued)

COUNTRY	YEAR OF CURRENT CONSTITUTION	UNITARY OR FEDERAL?	SEPARATION OF POWERS?	HEAD OF STATE	HEAD OF GOVERNMENT	STRUCTURE OF LEGISLATURE	JUDICIAL REVIEW?	ELECTORAL SYSTEM	PARTY SYSTEM
Iceland	1944	Unitary	No	Popularly elected largely ceremonial president	Prime minister elected by lower house of parliament	Unicameral, popularly elected	Supreme Court has some judicial review	Multimember proportional representation	Multi-party
Ireland	1937	Unitary	No	Popularly elected ceremonial president	Prime minister elected by lower house of parliament	Strongly asymmetric bicameralism; lower house popularly elected, upper house drawn from various sectors of society	Supreme Court has some judicial review	Multimember proportional representation	Two-party plus
India	1950	Federal, with twenty-eight states and seven "union territories"	No	Ceremonial president elected by parliament	Prime minister elected by lower house of parliament	Asymmetric bicameralism; lower house popularly elected, upper house chosen from states	Supreme Court has some judicial review	Single-member plurality	Multi-party
Israel	No written constitution	Unitary	No	Ceremonial president elected by parliament	Prime minister elected by lower house of parliament	Unicameral, popularly elected	Supreme Court has some judicial review	Proportional representation	Multi-party

Italy	1948	Unitary	Usually not, although Senate can sometimes check lower house and executive	Ceremonial president elected by parliament and regional delegates	Prime minister elected by lower house of parliament	Symmetric bicameralism, with members of both houses popularly elected	Constitutional court has some judicial review	Proportional representation	Multi-party
Japan	1947	Unitary	No	Hereditary ceremonial monarch	Prime minister elected by lower house of parliament	Asymmetric bicameral	Supreme Court has some judicial review	Mixed single-member plurality and proportional representation	Multi-party
Luxembourg	1868	Unitary	No	Hereditary ceremonial monarch	Prime minister elected by lower house of parliament	Unicameral, popularly elected	Supreme Court does not have judicial review	Proportional representation	Multi-party
Netherlands	1814	Unitary	No	Hereditary ceremonial monarch	Prime minister elected by lower house of parliament	Asymmetric bicameralism; lower house popularly elected, upper house elected by provinces	Supreme Court does not have judicial review	Proportional representation	Multi-party
New Zealand	No written constitution	Unitary	No	Ceremonial governor-general, appointed by prime minister, represents British monarch	Prime minister elected by lower house of parliament	Unicameral, popularly elected	Supreme Court does not have judicial review	Mixed single-member plurality and proportional representation	Two-party plus

Table 1 Comparison of twenty-two established democracies (continued)

COUNTRY	YEAR OF CURRENT CONSTITUTION	UNITARY OR FEDERAL?	SEPARATION OF POWERS?	HEAD OF STATE	HEAD OF GOVERNMENT	STRUCTURE OF LEGISLATURE	JUDICIAL REVIEW?	ELECTORAL SYSTEM	PARTY SYSTEM
Norway	1814	Unitary	No	Hereditary ceremonial monarch	Prime minister elected by lower house of parliament	Unicameral, popularly elected	Supreme Court has limited judicial review	Multimember proportional representation	Multi-party
Sweden	1975	Unitary	No	Hereditary ceremonial monarch	Prime minister elected by lower house of parliament	Unicameral, popularly elected	Supreme Court has limited judicial review	Multimember proportional representation	Multi-party
Switzerland	1874	Federal, with twenty-six cantons	Yes	Ceremonial president, rotating each year among Federal Council members	Seven-member Federal Council elected for fixed term by lower house of parliament	Symmetric bicameralism, both houses popularly elected	Supreme Court does not have judicial review	Proportional representation in lower house, single-member plurality in upper house	Multi-party

Note: This comparison table is based on the list of twenty-two democracies compiled by political scientists Arendt Lijphart, Robert Dahl, and others. It reflects countries that have been independent since 1950 and have experienced uninterrupted democracy since that time. As countries with a span of several decades of democratic self-government, these countries represent many of the most relevant points of comparison for the United States. Note that India is sometimes excluded from the list because of a state of emergency that was declared there between 1975 and 1977, although this was accomplished through existing constitutional mechanisms.

Table 2 An overview of U.S. politics and a comparative view

FEATURE	U.S. CHARACTERISTICS	COMPARATIVE VIEW
Nation, State, and Regime (Chapter 1)	The United States is a relatively new nation and state, but has a strong sense of national identity. The regime is defined by the Constitution, which is nearly as old as the state itself.	Many countries are rooted in ethnic identities that greatly predate their modern states; others are more modern creations like the United States. Most states have experienced several changes in regime.
Constitution (Chapter 2)	The U.S. Constitution is the oldest and longest continuously functioning such document, although quite brief and even vague.	Most constitutions are much longer and more detailed, are significantly changed or replaced more often, and enumerate social as well as political rights.
Federalism (Chapter 3)	The United States first introduced the idea of federalism, and both national and state governments have distinctive constitutional status and play active roles.	A number of large and/or diverse countries practice federalism, but about 7/8 of countries overall are unitary states with nearly all political power concentrated in the national capital.
Separation of Powers (Chapter 4)	The United States has a robust system of separation of powers with effective checks and balances among the executive, legislative, and judicial branches, each of which is largely autonomous of the others.	Parliamentary systems have no separation between legislative and executive authority. Many other countries with separation of powers, as in Latin America and Africa, tend to be strongly dominated by the executive.

Table 2   An overview of U.S. politics and a comparative view (continued)

FEATURE	U.S. CHARACTERISTICS	COMPARATIVE VIEW
The Executive Branch (Chapter 5)	The U.S. president is both the country's ceremonial head of state and hands-on head of government. Due to separation of powers, the president does not answer to Congress and can exercise significant powers unilaterally. The U.S. bureaucracy is comparatively small and dispersed among the national, state, and city levels.	Parliamentary systems have purely ceremonial heads of states, while prime ministers act as head of government as long as they control a parliamentary majority. Nondemocratic countries also tend to have very strong executives. Many developed countries, especially unitary states, have large, centralized bureaucracies that form a national elite.
The Legislative Branch (Chapter 6)	The upper and lower houses of the U.S. Congress, the Senate and the House of Representatives, have equal authority. Congress has a great deal of power, but this power is widely dispersed due to relatively weak parties, independent-minded members, and strong committees.	Most parliamentary systems have very strong lower houses but much weaker upper houses that mostly review and revise rather than initiate laws. Parliaments tend to be heavily dominated by the prime ministers they elect. In nondemocratic countries, legislatures usually play a consultative rather than governing role.
The Judicial Branch (Chapter 7)	The courts in the United States are an independent, coequal branch with the power of judicial review to strike down laws and executive acts as unconstitutional. Judges play an active role in the governing process.	Most court systems are more limited in their scope, dealing more with the case before them than with issuing broad legal rulings. Some countries have constitutional courts with judicial review, although few in practice can easily override executive or legislative acts.

Table 2 An overview of U.S. politics and a comparative view (continued)

FEATURE	U.S. CHARACTERISTICS	COMPARATIVE VIEW
Voting and Elections (Chapter 8)	The United States uses a single-member plurality system in which each elected office has its own election with a single winner: whoever gets the most votes.	Most countries use some form of proportional representation (PR), in which each election produces several winners from multiple parties based on percentage of the vote won.
Political Parties and Interest Groups (Chapter 9)	The United States has a stable, long-term two-party system. The two major parties are decentralized and relatively weak, unable to easily control their members. In part because of the weakness of parties, interest groups flourish in the United States, although they are not usually organized along lines of class.	Largely because of PR, most countries have multiple political parties that win votes and elect officials to office. These parties often have means to control their members and are more powerful than most interest groups, with the possible exception of organized labor.
Unconventional Participation (Chapter 10)	Since the Civil War, the United States has only rarely experienced political violence. Non-violent political protest has been more important, especially since the 1950s.	Many countries experience great political violence, with challengers seeking to overthrow the government or form a breakaway state. Political protest, both violent and nonviolent, is also common.
Political Values and Public Opinion (Chapter 11)	The United States has a long history of valuing self-reliance and personal independence, resulting in a comparatively low regard for big government. Americans are also more religious and patriotic than citizens in other developed countries.	Citizens of most developed countries tend to hold more liberal views on issues relating to religion and morality, are generally less nationalistic, and are more in favor of activist government. Views in some developing counties are closer to the United States in these areas.

I

The Constitutional Order

1

The American Nation, State, and Regime

Comparison is the basis of much of what we know about the world. Astronomers compare Earth with other planets to explain why the size of our globe and its distance from the sun allow life to flourish. Biologists study the physiology of other species for clues about how the human organism functions and how diseases can be combated. Economists often contrast the performance of one economy with reference to others, determining why some countries experience growth and prosperity while others encounter stagnation and poverty.

Political scientists also make use of comparisons; indeed, one entire subfield of the discipline is known as comparative politics. Through the close examination of the politics and government of many countries, it is possible to understand the strengths and weaknesses of different systems, and their ability or inability to offer stability, good governance, flexibility, deliberation, representation, and many other political values to their citizenry. These strengths and weaknesses are reflected in the historical development of many different dimensions of a political system, including its constitutional provisions, the configurations of its government institutions, the rules of its electoral system, and the political culture of its citizenry. All of these are among the topics that make up the theme of *The American Anomaly*.

In the pages ahead, it will become clear that U.S. politics and government are quite unusual and atypical, indeed even anomalous. This is not to say that there are one or two models in the world from which the United States deviates. Indeed, no country has a political system that is fully representative of the countries of the world, and many have some features even more anomalous than those found in the United States. Still, a comparative perspective can illuminate the full range of the ways in which the human race chooses to govern itself, as well as the gains, losses, and trade-offs that result from the different political institutions and processes that have developed in the United States.

To initiate this discussion, it is useful to start with three of the broadest concepts used in comparative politics to describe and categorize the political systems of different countries: *nation, state,* and *regime.*

The *nation* can be thought of as a form of collective identity among a group of people, generally rooted in a particular geographic location, and based on a set of shared cultural attributes such as religion, language, customs, and historical experience. Some nations, such as Japan and Ethiopia, have deep, even ancient, roots; others, such as Australia and Costa Rica, are comparatively recent creations. Likewise, many nations possess very robust and distinctive identities and a clear sense of their place in the world; China would fit into this category, long calling itself the "middle kingdom" because it viewed the Chinese nation as forming the very center of the world. By contrast, some other nations have a sense of nationhood that is more fragile or indistinct, such as Ukraine, which has long been overshadowed by its much larger neighbor Russia, with which it has innumerable historical and cultural links. The terms *ethnicity* or *ethnic group* are sometimes used more or less interchangeably with *nationality* or *nation.* (Note that in everyday use, the term *nation* is sometimes used synonymously with the word *country,* but the usage of the term here is a more technical and academic one.)

The second concept is the *state,* the term used to describe any of approximately 190 sovereign, independent countries in the world. Perhaps the simplest indicator of whether a political entity is regarded as a sovereign state within the international system is whether it has membership in the United Nations which, despite its name, is an organization composed of states (for a listing see <www.un.org/members>). By definition, sovereign states have no higher political authority above them and possess such characteristics as a specified land area, a permanent population, a monopoly on the legitimate use of violence within its borders, and the ability to enter into diplomatic relations with other states; this international system of states is often traced back to a pair of European treaties signed in 1648 called the

Peace of Westphalia. (The American states of the Union, for example, Vermont or Arizona, share sovereignty within the United States, but they are *not* states in the international sense.) When one particular national or ethnic group forms the large majority of a state, as is often but not always the case, it is termed a *nation-state*. Some nations, such as the Kurds of the Middle East and the Roma (Gypsies) of Europe, do not have their own state; some nations, most notably the Arab nation, are divided among multiple states. Further, some states, such as Malaysia and Afghanistan, are composed of multiple distinct ethnic groups.

The third concept is that of the *regime*, or the particular configuration of governing principles and institutions that prevail within any particular state. This term became widely familiar in the United States with regard to the 2003 invasion of Iraq, which had as its stated goal regime change in that country. Notably, when the regime led by the dictator Saddam Hussein and his Baathist Party was toppled by the U.S.-led invasion, Iraq's status as a sovereign state remained unchanged, although it was temporarily placed under U.S. occupation. Most regimes are legitimized by a written constitution that spells out how power is organized and allocated within the country. But even the most detailed constitutions rarely capture all the dimensions of how power is actually exercised, and many regimes distort or even disregard their constitutions when it is convenient to do so.

The incumbents of any particular regime—that is to say, those currently in public office or otherwise exercising power—are often referred to as the "government." Thus, for instance, the ten-year term of British Prime Minister Tony Blair is often called the "Blair government." In the United States, the term *government* refers to the entire multipart structure established under the Constitution; to specify the term of any one president, Americans are more likely to speak of presidential administrations, such as the Reagan Administration. Generally, however, the nation, state, and usually also the regime predates the individuals in power at any particular moment and also will outlast them.

Case Study: The Nation, State, and Regime in Poland

These three concepts overlap and intersect in a variety of ways, but in most cases each concept can be distinguished from the others. A useful example of these concepts is offered by the case of Poland. For at least a millennium, there has existed a distinctive Polish nation: a people who lived in a particular region of East-Central Europe and shared a number of cultural characteristics, such as use of a distinctive Slavic language written with Roman letters and a fervent brand of Roman Catholicism. For many years, the Polish nation, under their king, was part of a multiethnic state. This state disappeared in the 1790s when Poland was partitioned by the Prussian, Hapsburg, and Russian Empires and effectively vanished from political maps for a century and a half. During this time the Polish nation, however, endured and it was able to reassert its political sovereignty when Poland was reestablished after World War I as a nation-state.

At that time, the Poles attempted to create a new democratic regime based on a written constitution led by the government of President Jan Pilsudski. But that regime proved unstable, and soon Poland was sequentially invaded and occupied by the German Nazi Army and the Soviet Red Army. After World War II, the Soviet Union occupied Poland and imposed a new regime that drew its authority from Communist doctrine and, more importantly, the threat of Soviet invasion. This new regime did not alter the basic identity of the Polish nation or state, however, but simply represented one more phase in a historical succession of regimes. In the 1980s, the last government of the Communist regime, led by General Wojciech Jaruszelski, took extreme measures to repress the burgeoning Solidarity trade union movement. The fall of the Berlin Wall and the collapse of Communism in Eastern Europe in 1989, however, led to the creation of today's restored democratic regime, with its first government led by Solidarity leader Lech Walesa.

The American Nation

The interrelationships among the American nation, state, regime, and government are not quite as clear as they are in the case of Poland. Unlike Poland and many other nations of Europe and Asia, the United States has a comparatively short history upon which to draw its sense of nationhood. Indeed, the United States has been termed the "first new nation" because it achieved independence from its mother country before any other major colony did so and because its national identity was largely self-invented.

This new American nation, of necessity, had to draw upon different markers of identity than older nations such as Denmark or Korea with long histories, distinct languages, and well-established national identities. First off, the more than 99 percent of Americans who are not Native Americans clearly cannot make a claim that their ancestors have inhabited the land since prehistoric times. This is true of most countries in the western hemisphere, although some, such as Guatemala and Bolivia, forged national identities with a strong component from their much larger population of indigenous peoples.

Cultural attributes also do not provide a clear path to a distinctively American national identity. Although the English language does help to unify the country, English is obviously not unique to the United States and many Americans speak English poorly or not at all. Americans also do not share a single religious tradition; indeed religious diversity and nonconformity is an American hallmark. American art, architecture, and high culture—whether the neoclassical dome and monumental sculptures of the U.S. Capitol Building or the gothic spires and stained glass windows of the National Cathedral—likewise have their roots elsewhere. And the great ethnic and racial mixture that makes up the Americans population renders moot any notion of shared ancestry, except perhaps in the broadest sense of a shared humanity.

Thus, the usual cultural, religious, and linguistic markers that might help to distinguish, say, the Polish nation from its neighbors, are mostly not in place in the United States. Nonetheless, the United States does have a robust civic identity of its own, often forged in the crucible of conflict and violence. Major historical events, especially the Revolution and the Civil War, have provided the country with a pantheon of national heroes such as George Washington, Thomas Jefferson, and Abraham Lincoln. Other developments, such as the struggle against slavery and segregation, the westward expansion, the experience of immigration, recovery from the Great Depression, and victory in World War II and the Cold War, have contributed to a national sense of purpose and progress, led again by towering figures such as Franklin Delano Roosevelt, Martin Luther King, Jr., and increasingly in popular opinion, Ronald Reagan. Through all of these phases, a panoply of images, symbols, and ideas have formed the basis for a common national identity, including founding documents such as the Declaration of Independence and the Constitution; the American flag and the national anthem and pledge of allegiance that honor it; and iconic buildings and monuments such as the Statue of Liberty, Mount Rushmore, and the Vietnam War Memorial. Thus, although Americans lack the ancient roots of many nations in Europe, Asia, or the Middle East, they nonetheless have a very clear sense of who they are as a people—a distinctive sense of nationhood.

Much of this national identity has always been based upon a specific set of principles and ideas, sometimes collectively called the "American Creed." In a feat that was at the time unique in world history, the founding generation in the United States drew upon political philosophy and their own practical experience in colonial and state government to first lay out and then to implement sweeping principles by which the United States would be governed. These principles revolve around protection of individual liberty and freedom from tyranny: as a goal established in the Declaration of Independence, as the motivating force behind the design of the Constitution, as the recurrent concern—even obsession—that animates the Federalist Papers.

The subsequent history of the United States served to reinforce the centrality of individual liberty and freedom from tyranny, especially when compared with the perceived corruption of the Old World. The first settlers had had to cultivate a philosophy of total self-reliance in the absence of preexisting governmental or social structures. This ethos was reinforced throughout the westward expansion of the early to mid-nineteenth century, which was viewed as the manifest destiny of the American nation. Then again throughout the late nineteenth and early twentieth centuries, the United States welcomed millions of self-motivated immigrants who arrived in the United States to make their own way in the world. These new arrivals were welcomed as full-fledged new Americans as long as they pledged fealty to the Constitution and the principles it embodied. In such an environment of capitalism, democracy, and egalitarianism, the United States viewed itself as a model for the world, "the last best hope of mankind." That the United States was a society which abused the rights of African Americans, Native Americans and others is, today at least, usually viewed as a great shortcoming rather than a contradiction of the principles of liberty. And since 1865, the arc of U.S. history has been toward greater participation and individual freedom of the entire citizenry, slowly as that arc may move at times.

The Development of Nationhood

Among the other new nations of the western hemisphere, some have a strong sense of nationhood, while others do not. Like the United States, Mexico has a unique and distinctive culture and national identity, and a clear sense of its place in history and in the world. Drawing upon the historical memory of such traumatic experiences as the conquest—yet endurance—of the indigenous population, the struggle for independence from Spain, and the revolution against the established elites in the early twentieth century, Mexico has forged a strong civic identity that draws upon both native and European roots. With one quarter of the world's Spanish-speaking population, Mexico also plays a leading cultural role among Latin American nations without submerging its identity into this broader community.

Canada, on the other hand, offers one of the clearest examples of a country where a history of evolutionary rather than revolutionary change has helped to make the question of national identity a perennial preoccupation. Spared the experience of bloody revolution, civil war, or even major internal strife, English-speaking Canadians have had to rely on the incremental development of an independent identity from Great Britain, whose Queen remains the Canadian head of state. Although their territory is vast, Canadians are so hemmed in by inhospitable climate and terrain that more than 80 percent of the population lives in a thin strip of land within 200 miles of the U.S. border, further diluting the development of a distinctive national identity. As one famous quip puts it, "Canada has too much geography and not enough history." Today, Canadians (outside Quebec) are wracked by questions about who they are as a people, and about how they are distinct from the British and, especially, from Americans.

In Australia and New Zealand, comparable evolutionary historical processes have led to similar questions. Neither country ever experienced a revolution or a civil war, and both also retain the British Queen as their head of state. With only small indigenous minority populations, both countries traditionally viewed themselves as outposts of the British Empire, maintaining the English language and European culture; some remark that New Zealanders particularly are "more British than the British." Over the past fifty years, however, the end of the British Empire, an influx of non-European immigrants, and the economic rise of Asian countries have forced these two nations into an identity crisis over whether they are still essentially transplanted European societies or distinctive Oceanic countries with strong linkages to neighboring cultures.

It should be noted that a revolutionary tradition is not essential to the development of a strong sense of nationhood among new nations. The French-speaking, largely Roman Catholic Quebecois of Canada have no revolutionary tradition per se—indeed, Quebec absorbed many highly counterrevolutionary influences when conservative nobility and clergymen fled there after the French Revolution. Still, Quebec enjoys a robust sense of its own nationhood sharpened by centuries of domination by English-speaking Protestants. One of the distinctive features of modern Canadian politics is the perennial question of whether Quebec should become an independent state— through, of course, peaceful means.

Conversely, Argentina has a revolutionary tradition and powerful patriotic symbolism, such as its much-revered sky blue and white flag, but remains paralyzed in part by confusion over its fundamental identity. Located on the South American continent but with a tiny indigenous population, is it a Latin country like Peru or Brazil, or is it fundamentally a nation of Italian, German, Spanish, and other European immigrants? With an educated populace, a developed infrastructure, and bountiful natural resources but recurrent political and economic instability, is it part of the developed world or the developing world? Some have argued that Argentina's twentieth century experience of rule by charismatic figures such as President Juan Peron and his wife Evita, and also by a string of military dictators, is caused in part by a national desire for clear direction and decisive leadership.

The American State and Regime

An unusual characteristic of the United States is that its state and its regime are very closely linked, indeed almost synonymous. In most countries, the state has existed for longer than any particular regime, and many states have seen a number of different regimes over time. Americans, however, have lived under the same regime now since 1789, the year that the U.S. Constitution took effect just seven years after the thirteen American colonies achieved full independence from Great Britain. Although it has been formally amended more than two dozen times and also significantly reinterpreted during crises such as the Civil War, the Great Depression, and the Civil Rights Movement, the essential elements of the Constitutional framework have endured for more than two centuries. (The U.S. Constitution is discussed in much more detail in the following chapter.)

To a degree that is quite anomalous, then, the United States as a state is largely defined by its Constitution. For instance, the presidential oath of office includes a promise to "preserve, protect, and defend" the Constitution, and naturalizing citizens must swear to take up arms, if needed, to "defend the Constitution." This fusion of the state and the regime can best be seen in the single term *The Republic* as used in the Pledge of Allegiance. When school children, new citizens, attendees at sporting events, and others pledge allegiance "to the flag, and to the Republic for which it stands," they are affirming their support simultaneously both for the United States as a sovereign state and for the regime that was established by the Constitution in 1789.

In contrast, some countries have had so many different regimes that they have adopted a numbering system. France, for instance, currently counts itself as in its Fifth Republic since its monarchy was overthrown by the revolution of 1789, a year in which France as a state and as a nation was already centuries old. Yet this enumeration does not even include other nonrepublican regimes that have ruled France, such as under the Emperor Napoleon and under a military government during World War II. Perhaps the most notorious example of a numbering system of regimes would be the Nazi's use of "Third Reich" to denote the third German empire. By that reckoning, the current Federal Republic of Germany would be that country's fourth regime (or its fifth if the inter-war Weimar Republic is counted).

Further, as the example of Germany demonstrates, any one state may have been under the control of multiple, different types of regimes. One key element in defining a type of regime is what it draws upon as the source of its authority and legitimacy—what gives it the right to govern its people. The First and Second Reichs in Germany are examples of *traditional* regimes in that the wellspring of their authority was a hereditary monarchy and aristocracy. In such traditional regimes, rulers have the right to rule because they have always had that right (or have at least had it for a long period of time). Today, many of the monarchies of the Middle East, such as in Jordan, Morocco, and Saudi Arabia, retain powerful kings who exert a right to rule because they inherited it from their fathers and sometimes also because of their descent from the Prophet Mohammed or their role as protectors of holy sites.

The Nazi's Third Reich in Germany offers a quintessential example of a *totalitarian* regime. As the name suggests, these regimes seek (even if they cannot always actually achieve) total control over all aspects of the lives of their people, whose principal role is to work for and support the goals of the state. In seeking to regulate all aspects of their citizen's lives, totalitarian regimes try to destroy, or at least to completely subordinate, any institutions that might intervene between individuals and the power of the state, such as political parties, trade unions, churches, and even families. To seek such absolute control, totalitarian regimes often root their claims of authority in all-encompassing ideologies, such as the sweeping Nazi vision of Aryan racial supremacy.

Other major examples of totalitarian regimes have drawn not on racial identity but on class struggle as their unifying ideology in the form of Communism. The Soviet Union under Stalin and the People's Republic of China under Mao were strongly totalitarian regimes, and North Korea under the Kim dynasty is as totalitarian as any country in history. Some other non-Communist regimes may also fall into the totalitarian category by virtue of their claims to rule based on religion, particularly Islam; the former Taliban regime in Afghanistan and, at times, postrevolutionary Iran come to mind.

Milder but somewhat similar to totalitarian regimes are *authoritarian* regimes that usually lack a totalizing ideology but instead base their right to rule on more pragmatic claims to authority. These regimes will usually not attempt to regulate and direct all aspects of the personal and professional lives of their citizenry, but will expect them to defer to the regime on political questions. Such regimes may draw on many different sources of authority. Some might claim to have brought order or prosperity to the society, as in the case of contemporary China under Deng Xiaoping and his successors and Russia under President Vladimir Putin. Often authoritarian regimes draw upon simple brute force wrapped in patriotic language, as has been the case in countless military-backed regimes in Latin America, Asia, and Africa.

With regard to the United States, totalitarianism is an alien concept, although a case could be made that under slavery and segregation, African Americans were subjected to a form of near-totalitarian control under a totalizing ideology of white supremacy. As for authoritarianism, the U.S. government has occasionally exerted an extraordinary degree of authority during times of crisis, civil strife, or foreign war. During the U.S. Civil War, for instance, Abraham Lincoln suspended some civil liberties. During World War II, Franklin D. Roosevelt ordered the internment of Japanese Americans and largely took command of the economy in order to focus it on military production. But such exercises of authoritarianism have occurred only in exceptional, and very limited, periods within the U.S. experience. Indeed, one of the most enduring features of U.S. politics has been a recurrent fear of excessive concentration of power, stretching from the preoccupation of the Founders with separating, checking, and balancing power to the recent resistance from the courts, Congress, and public opinion to

President George W. Bush's attempts to expand the scope of executive authority.

More representative of the U.S. experience are *democratic* regimes, which draw their authority from the people. The mandate of the people generally is provided in the form of free, fair, and competitive elections, but also from other types of citizen input such as public opinion, social movements, and interest group activity. While democratic regimes may share a common source of authority, often called "popular sovereignty" or the "consent of the governed," there are many different forms that democratic political systems can take. Indeed, a major theme of this volume is that the U.S. model of government and politics is no more or no less inherently democratic than many other systems. (For one organization's analysis of which states are democratic, visit <www.freedomhouse.org> and click on Map of Freedom.)

Unusual Characteristics of the United States

While much of the politics and government of the United States can be explained in terms of its historical experience and institutional structures, other factors also play significant roles. To a degree not always appreciated by American citizens, the United States is a highly atypical country: far larger, more populous, richer, and ultimately more powerful than almost all of the 190 other independent countries of the world. Its various attributes taken together arguably make the United States the most anomalous country in the world.

To begin, consider geography. At some 3.8 million square miles, the United States covers one-sixteenth of the world's surface and is the third largest country in the world, following only Russia and Canada and just ahead of China, Brazil, and Australia. The United States is, in fact, about fourteen times larger than the average country of the world, with most of the states (outside of Alaska) being easily habitable territory. The United States is also enormously diverse geographically, encompassing large swaths of deserts in the Southwest, several major mountain ranges, fertile farmlands, huge open prairies, and thousands of miles of coastline, features that offer abundant natural resources. This bounty has enabled the U.S. population to expand seemingly without limit, hemmed in neither by vast outback desert as in Australia, by expanses of arctic tundra as in Canada and Russia, nor impenetrable jungle as in Brazil. It has also provided enormous economic benefits in the form of a huge common market with the resources to be nearly self-sustaining, barring such problematic imports as oil.

Alongside such scale and scope, the United States possesses an unusual degree of geographical isolation, having only two directly contiguous countries, although several small island nations are also nearby. For at least a century and a half, none of these countries has posed a significant direct threat to U.S. interests (although Cuba has certainly tried). In the age of intercontinental ballistic missiles and terrorism, this isolation is no longer as great as it has been at some points in history, but the legacy of isolation remains significant today and was crucial in the shaping of American political history. Compare this with, for instance, Poland, which today has a land or sea border with twelve different countries, several of them historical antagonists.

If the United States is vastly large, it is also highly populated. As with geography, it places third in the world, more populous than all but China and India, and well ahead of Indonesia, Russia, and Brazil. With 300 million people, the United States has about ten times the average population of countries of the world. Compared with such population giants as China and India (which each have nearly four times the U.S. population), however, the population density of the United States is relatively low and widely scattered across its territory. The average population density of the world is 43 people per square kilometer, but the figure in the United States is only 30 people—compared with France at 110, Britain at 243, and Taiwan at 636.

Combining geography and population, then, provides the United States with a highly unusual profile among countries: the United States is both exceptionally large and populous, yet also highly diverse and decentralized. But the unique characteristics do not end there: it is also the only country that is large, highly populated, *and* wealthy. This is a combination that is wholly anomalous in the world; other large countries are either populous but relatively poor (China, India, Russia, Brazil) or wealthy but relatively unpopulated (Canada, Australia). The United States has thus been able to construct an economy based on both a large population, offering a huge internal market of both laborers and consumers, and a diverse and well-endowed continental land mass. Further, the United States has largely been spared the devastation of war, whether originating from outside or within the United States. Even such major incidents as the bombing of Pearl Harbor in 1941 and the terrorist attacks of September 11, 2001, inflicted damage that was localized and minor compared with the destruction of full-scale armed conflict. And despite domestic crises such as the Great Depression and the upheavals of the 1960s, the United States has not seen truly crippling internal strife since the American Civil War ended in 1865.

These three major endowments – large population, extensive territory, and geographic isolation – have contributed to producing the most impressive economy in the world today, and perhaps in history. In a global economy of approximately $60 trillion per year, the United States accounts for about one fifth or $12.5 trillion. While the European Union collectively accounts for slightly more, the United States far outstrips all other individual countries, with its nearest competitor being Japan at $4.5 trillion. The U.S. economy is so large that it exceeds the next six countries following Japan—Germany, China, Britain, France, Italy, and Canada—*combined*. And this figure is not simply because the United States has a large population: per capita gross domestic product (GDP) is $42,000, fifth in the world behind Luxembourg, Norway, the United Arab Emirates, and Equatorial Guinea. Most European countries have GDPs between $25,000 and $35,000, with the European Union average at $28,000.

As the inclusion of the African state of Equatorial Guinea suggests, not all countries have an equitable distribution of wealth; most residents of Equatorial Guinea live in poverty while a few families control huge oil reserves. Compared with other rich countries, wealth in the United States is dispersed in highly unequal patterns. In one ranking of 124 countries in terms of income inequality, the United States placed 92nd, well behind every other developed country in the world. The top 10 percent in the United States earns 16 times more than the bottom 10 percent; this is double the level of inequality found in the most equal country, Denmark, and in close company with the Philippines, Cameroon, and Nicaragua. Poverty is also heavily concentrated in certain populations, such as ethnic and racial minorities, and certain regions, such as Appalachia and the rural Great Plains.

Also, the overall size of the U.S. economy is useful in projecting what have been termed hard power and soft power throughout the world. Hard power refers to military strength, which has been totally unmatched since at least the collapse of the Soviet Union in 1991. The United States has more than 700 military bases, located on every continent except Antarctica, and in 2005 the United States spent about $520 billion on the military—roughly equal to the next fifty countries combined. Military strength, combined with economic muscle, provides the United States with enormous nonmilitary soft power, such as diplomatic leverage that allows it to very heavily influence—and sometimes to dominate—both other countries and multilateral institutions such as the United Nations, the International Monetary Fund, and the World Bank. Another form of soft power is the influence of American popular culture. Originating within the United States' large internal market for entertainment, U.S. films, music, television, fashion, fads, and other forms of popular culture have a huge impact on audiences and consumers throughout the world. Through the projection of both hard and soft power, the United States has become very familiar to citizens of other nations. All of these factors mean that, of necessity, the rest of the world pays far more attention to the United States than the United States pays to them.

Conclusion

Educated citizens outside the United States often live in proximity to and interact with countries, cultures, and languages other than their own, broadening their awareness of how different and diverse countries can be. Living in a comparatively isolated, often inward-focused nation, many Americans are aware neither of the range of variation found among the countries of the world nor of how anomalous the United States is when viewed comparatively. The focus of this book is specifically on the diverse forms of politics and government that can be found throughout the world. Learning about this diversity is a valuable goal in itself, but is also an important way to understand American politics and government in comparative perspective.

Further Reading

- *The First New Nation: The United States in Historical and Comparative Perspective.* Seymour Martin Lipset. Transaction Publishers, New York: 2003.
- *On Democracy.* Robert Dahl. Yale University Press, New Haven, CT: 2001.
- *America the Unusual.* John Kingdon. Bedford/St. Martin's, New York: 1999.

Web-Based Exploration Exercise

Visit the *CIA World Factbook* (<www.cia.gov/cia/publications/factbook/index.html>) and use the drop-down menu to access statistics about the United States. Select any four significant facts about the United States, choosing one fact each from the sections on Geography, People, Government, and Economy. Then select any three other countries, and compare them with the United States in terms of the same facts. Ideally, the three countries you choose should be diverse in terms of government type, geographic region, or other characteristics. What do you think might account for these differences?

Question for Debate and Discussion

This chapter lays out the basic case that the United States is so anomalous, so different from other countries, that a comparative perspective can illuminate features of American politics and government that can otherwise get overlooked or taken for granted. What is the practical value of such comparisons? Why and to what extent do you think the U.S. political system should seek to change itself to more closely resemble other political systems? To what degree do you think significant changes are even possible?

2
THE U.S. CONSTITUTION

When it was devised and enacted between 1787 and 1789, the U.S. Constitution was a true anomaly. Until that point, political systems throughout the world had generally just evolved over time, reacting to changing circumstances with little prior thought or planning. Indeed, the constitutional planning of the founding era was the first time in history that a group of national leaders, in this case delegates from the thirteen American states, took on the explicit challenge of codifying a new political structure to govern their country and writing it down in a single document. The framers fused abstract concepts such as the "consent of the governed" and "limited government" with pragmatic considerations about how to garner popular support in enough states to ensure ratification. In ways unanticipated by the framers, the Constitution has endured with only fairly small textual changes for over 215 years, making it the longest continuously functioning written constitution in the world.

Today, the concept of deliberate constitution writing seems unremarkable. Indeed, the world has seen several successive waves of similar deliberations, such as after the collapse of empires during World War I, during the period of global decolonization after World War II, and following the end of the Cold War in the 1990s. Many of the constitutional structures created after these epochal events took forms quite different from the U.S. system, but the very idea of writing a constitutional document itself draws strongly upon the American precedent.

While the U.S. Constitution may be a global prototype, it also contains numerous elements that are relatively unique. Unlike more recent constitutions, it is exceptionally brief, sometimes to the point of vagueness, consisting of just some 4400 words in the original text. This brevity adds a great deal of ambiguity into the meaning of the document, the text of which is quite difficult to change. This helps to explain why the Bill of Rights (Amendments 1–10) and some other Amendments provide many explicit protections of political rights, but they are virtually silent on the social and economic rights found in many later constitutions. The arduous amendment process also helps to explain why a number of anachronistic provisions, born of pragmatic compromises in the 1780s, still remain in force today.

Case Study: The South African Constitution of 1996

One of the starkest contrasts with the U.S. Constitution is the constitution of the Republic of South Africa enacted in 1996. While this document may be no more representative of constitutions as a whole than is the U.S. Constitution, it presents an extreme case against which the American document can be considered. This 1996 Constitution replaced an interim document created in 1993 as part of the peaceful evolution toward majority control after decades under the brutal system of apartheid, in which power was reserved to the white minority. In some ways the South African constitutional process paralleled the development of a multicolored, complexly patterned new national flag, which was often criticized as jumbled and inelegant, but which reflected the valid and compelling interests of multiple elements within the society. Indeed, one of the express purposes of the new South African Constitution is to "heal the divisions of the past and establish a society based on democratic values, social justice and fundamental human rights."

One notable characteristic is the document's length. The original text of the U.S. Constitution contains just a short preamble and seven fairly brief articles that can be printed in as little as five pages, with a few more pages for the twenty-seven Amendments. But the South African constitution runs to 140 pages and includes fourteen chapters consisting of 243 sections, plus an additional seven lengthy schedules. As might be expected, the document establishes the branches of government, such as the presidency, the parliament, and the supreme court. It also establishes many of the basic political rights seen in the U.S. Constitution, including freedom of religion, belief and opinion, expression, assembly, association, property, and political participation, as well as guarantees of legal due process and prohibitions on slavery.

The most striking aspect of the South African constitution, however, is its broad ranging social guarantees, which have led some to call it the most progressive in the world. For instance, it acknowledges ten official languages and encourages the promotion of three other African languages, eight languages spoken among immigrant communities, three languages used in religious services, and sign language for the hearing impaired. By contrast, the U.S. Constitution never mentions language, and the United States has no official language, notwithstanding the historical predominance of English.

Likewise, where the Fourteenth Amendment to the U.S. Constitution briefly and vaguely provides for "equal protection of the law," the South African Constitution specifies nondiscrimination on the basis of "race, gender, sex, pregnancy, marital status, ethnic or social origin, color, sexual orientation, age, disability, religion, conscience, belief, culture, language and birth." Explicit protections are offered for "the right to bodily and psychological integrity," including reproductive rights. And rights are guaranteed in areas as diverse as the formation of unions, living in a safe environment, health care, food, water, social security, education, and even access to information held by the state.

Although the legacy of apartheid, the persistence of poverty, the AIDS epidemic, and many other factors limit the ability of South Africa to enforce many of these provisions, their very existence makes that country's constitution a starkly different document than its American counterpart, and one with real-world consequences. For instance, in 2005 the Supreme Court of South Africa ruled that the Constitution's specific ban on discrimination based on sexual orientation required the legalization of same-sex marriage. After some discussion, Parliament the next year extended full marriage equality to all of its citizens, making South Africa the first jurisdiction outside of North America and Western Europe to do so.

The U.S. Constitution: Brevity and Vagueness

Although the U.S. Constitution is both brief and, at times, quite vague, it is far more meaningful than those of some countries with elaborate, formal documents that are not worth the paper on which they are printed. The 1972 constitution of North Korea, for instance, lavishes rights to freedom of speech, the press, assembly, association, demonstration, religion, and rest upon the "workers, peasants, soldiers, and working intellectuals," all of whom are in fact subject to the whims of the brutal dictatorship of the Kim dynasty. Still other countries may have constitutions that their governments are too weak to actually enforce in all or part of the national territory; notable cases in this category would be "failed states" such as Somalia and Afghanistan, where regional warlords wield most power outside the capital city.

Among democratic states, the U.S. Constitution is, of course, much more specific than the unwritten constitutions of some democracies. The term *unwritten* is actually misleading because the constitutions of these countries may incorporate many important written documents, such as acts of parliament or international treaties. In such systems, however, the constitution is not a single document but the composite result of a long evolutionary tradition in which some conventions and precedents have become so well established that they are considered binding even in the absence of a single authoritative document. This is particularly the case in countries of the British parliamentary tradition, especially the United Kingdom and New Zealand. Strikingly, in some of these systems, the single most important political figure—the prime minister—is rarely if ever mentioned in constitutional documents. Indeed, the shifting power relationships among the monarch, the prime minister, the cabinet of ministers, the speaker of the House of Commons, and the rank-and-file members of Parliament have never been explicitly codified, but it is nonetheless quite clearly established in each of those countries. The other prominent example of a democracy with an unwritten constitution is Israel, where nine basic laws establish the outline of the political system, augmented at times by Jewish laws and customs. Despite ongoing discussion, disagreements among various religious, ethnic, and political factions in Israel have precluded consensus on a single authoritative constitutional document.

Within the realm of written constitutions, the text of the U.S. Constitution is quite lacking in detail, as noted in the comparison with the South Africa constitution (which is actually not the most extreme: the 1950 Constitution of India contains 395 articles divided into 22 parts with 12 schedules and 3 appendices). The U.S. Constitution has sometimes been called a "citizen's charter" in that it is intended more to set a process in motion than to carefully identify and provide for all contingencies. In part, this is because the very act of writing up a national constitution was a novel concept in the 1780s (although it did draw very heavily on earlier experience with enacting state-level constitutions as well as the Articles of Confederation that ineffectually governed the United States between 1781 and 1789). The framers were not always sure what they wanted in the new constitution and had few relevant precedents upon which to draw in creating such features as a democratic bicameral legislature, an elected executive, and a national judiciary.

As a result, a number of crucial features of the American political system are nowhere to be found in the text of the Constitution. The sprawling structure of committees and subcommittees of Congress that are so indispensable to its work are only vaguely implied in the fleeting provision of Article I that "each House may determine the rules of its proceedings." The crucial division of each chamber into two party caucuses, which determine the leadership of both chambers and the chairs of all committees, is also entirely unmentioned. In fact, political parties are completely absent from the Constitution even though they are absolutely central to the organization of Congress, as well as to elections and many other features of American political life.

Similarly, Article II clearly gives the president the power to appoint "heads of the executive departments" (subject to Senate confirmation). But nowhere does it explicitly provide the power to direct them once in office, reassign them, or fire them; these powers became established only through actual practice and later court rulings. Article III, creating the Supreme Court, is perhaps the vaguest article. In fact, the Court's single greatest power, the ability to review and overturn acts by congress and the president, is never explicitly stated. Although implied in early constitutional discussion, judicial review was not articulated and established until the 1803 legal case of *Marbury v. Madison.*

The Process of Constitutional Change

The brevity and vagueness of the U.S. Constitution has meant that throughout history, it has been exceptionally subject to interpretation by citizens, by the President, by Congress, and most of all by the federal courts. On the one hand, this has provided the flexibility needed for a single document to endure for over 200 years, during which time the country expanded from the shores of the Atlantic Ocean across the North American continent and changed from a preindustrial, agricultural society to a postindustrial, information-age economy.

On the other hand, the vagueness of the Constitution has allowed competing political forces to make seemingly equally legitimate constitutional claims, leading to sharp conflict. Early in the Republic, both proponents and opponents of slavery could argue that the Constitution was on their side, precisely because it was largely silent on the issue. During the Civil War, both the Union and the Confederacy could claim that their view of states' rights (as well as slavery) was the one promulgated by the Constitution. During both the Progressive Era and the Great Depression, the Constitution was invoked both by those who opposed government regulation of the economy, because such powers are not specifically enumerated in the text, and by those who sought a vigorous role for a government in meeting the changing needs of an industrializing, urbanizing country. More recently, the civil liberties and civil rights guarantees of various Constitutional amendments went from a minimalist interpretation in the 1950s to one ensuring far broader protections by the 1970s. Today, a major fault line in debates over the Constitution is whether it is best understood as a steadily evolving, living document that adapts to the times, or if it is a static legal instrument that must be interpreted solely in the light of the original intent of the framers.

Such a process of adaptation and accommodation is also commonly found in countries with unwritten constitutions, where all that is needed is an act of parliament for sweeping constitutional change. For example, New Zealand eliminated its provinces in 1875 and abolished the upper house of its parliament in 1950, all by a simple majority vote of parliament. Similarly, in the late 1990s, the British government enacted far-reaching constitutional changes, again all with a simple majority vote of the House of Commons. Among the major innovations were removing most hereditary nobility from their seats in the House of Lords; establishing regional legislatures in Scotland, Wales, and Northern Ireland; and expanding local self-governance in the great metropolis of London.

In countries with written constitutions, however, new interpretations are much more likely to be integrated directly into the text of the constitution through some more or less complicated process. Indeed, in some cases, countries simply scrap their old constitutions and approve entirely new ones. When the parliamentary government created by the French constitution of 1946 proved weak and unstable, an entirely new constitution with a much stronger executive was enacted just 12 years later. This was possible because unlike in the United States, the French regime and the French state are not closely associated, with the long history of the state encompassing many successive monarchical, revolutionary, imperial, democratic, and other regimes. Other countries have experienced many more changes of constitution, sometimes within the space of a few years; in the twentieth century, Ecuador has had six different constitutions, Haiti has had seven, Nigeria has had eight, and Ghana has had nine. Such frequent changes in constitutions are usually reflective of a volatile political situation with frequent shifts in power, in which new constitutions may become little more than justifications for those who seize power by military or other illegal means.

It is technically possible in the American system to promulgate a new constitution via a Constitutional Convention called by three-quarters of the states, but the ever-growing weight of history creates a huge disincentive for such a step. A Constitutional Convention would likely be a chaotic process, if only because there are so many more divergent voices in American politics today than at the time of the founding. Thus, any new constitution would probably more closely resemble the detailed law code of the South African document than the lean quality of the existing U.S. Constitution. (Many U.S. state constitutions, which are much more easily amended or replaced than the federal Constitution, are long, convoluted documents.) It is also widely, and almost certainly correctly, assumed that any new constitution, shorn of the weight of history, could never command the respect and deference that the Constitution of 1789 enjoys.

Of course, part of the reason that there has never been a need for a new Constitutional Convention is that the framers established another, quite brilliant, solution to the question of formal textual change. Article V provides for amendments on any constitutional issue (with the exception of equal representation for each state in the U.S. Senate). However, Article V deliberately makes an amendment quite difficult: two thirds of the members of each house of Congress must approve an amendment, followed by ratification by three quarters of the states, generally through a vote in the state legislatures. Such a high threshold, or supermajority requirement, guarantees that only those amendments that enjoy enormous consensus in the country will actually be enacted. Although the Constitution was not framed in terms of political parties, the two thirds requirements in Congress mean that amendments require significant bipartisan support to make it out of Congress, as well as broad support across a wide variety of states.

The requirement of supermajority support in the national legislature for constitutional amendment is a common feature of written constitutional systems, with the necessary percentage usually varying from three fifths to two thirds. It is also common that when a country has a bicameral legislature, both houses must approve the bill. In Brazil, for instance, amendments take effect if just 60 percent of both houses vote to ratify on two separate occasions, meaning that a relatively small legislative majority can make enormous changes after each election. (However, certain provisions are shielded from changes, and amendments cannot be introduced during times of political crisis.) In some countries, particularly those with a single legislative chamber such as the Nordic states, an additional restraint is added by requiring two consecutive sessions of the legislature to approve the amendment, meaning that any given legislative majority must have earned reelection by the people at least once.

Many countries, like the United States, require a second step of ratification after action by the national legislature. One common form in federal states is to require support by a majority vote in some proportion of the provinces, such as half in the case of Mexico and two-thirds in Ethiopia. Another method is to submit the amendment to a direct vote of the people via a referendum either automatically, as is the case in Ireland and Japan, or following the request of some actor in the system, such as the president, a percentage of legislators, some proportion of provinces, or a prescribed number of voters. Australia goes further still by requiring a double majority of half the population and at least four of its six states.

The U.S. requirements for amendment are not the most arduous in the world; Argentina, for instance, must convene a constitutional convention to enact an amendment. But the U.S. system of amendment remains unusually difficult and would be perhaps ill-suited for countries with highly detailed constitutions that require frequent fine-tuning and adaptation. The threshold of three quarters of the states (thirty-eight of the fifty) is high in itself, but ratification requires a majority vote in both houses of the legislature in the forty-nine states that practice bicameralism (Nebraska is the sole exception). Thus, opponents of an amendment need only to defeat it, or even to keep it from coming to a vote, in just one chamber in thirteen states (out of a total of ninety-nine chambers in fifty states) to prevent the amendment from taking effect. This helps to explain why over 10,000 amendments have been proposed to Congress throughout American history but only twenty-seven have actually been ratified; just seventeen of which have been since 1791.

Anachronistic Elements of the U.S. Constitution

In part because of the difficulty of the amending process, historical features of the U.S. Constitution have remained in place that, at best, are of questionable value and, at worst, may be viewed as antidemocratic. The most obvious in this regard is that each state of the Union is guaranteed equal representation in the U.S. Senate regardless of its population, one of the pragmatic compromises that made possible the ratification of the Constitution. This feature of the Senate is discussed in more detail in Chapter 6, but it is hard to make a democratic argument that the roughly half million people of Wyoming should have the same number of U.S. Senators as the nearly 37 million citizens of California. Another oddity in the U.S. Constitution, reviewed at greater length in Chapter 8, is the Electoral College. This method for selecting a president is cumbersome and peculiar, and as the American people learned in 2000, it is possible for the candidate who received the most popular support to not become president. Yet neither of these anomalies has ever been addressed, in part because these provisions empower smaller (i.e., less populous) states, whose support would be needed to pass a constitutional amendment. Given the extremely high supermajority requirements for amendment, representatives of about 3 percent of the U.S. population, if they all worked together, could block a constitutional change favored by the representatives of the other 97 percent of the country.

The other major area of the U.S. Constitution that remains anomalous, even anachronistic, is the near-total absence of any mention of social and economic protections. The example of the South African Constitution may be extreme in its articulation of numerous, detailed rights, but most constitutions contain at least some provisions about the health and well-being of the citizenry. The 1991 constitution of the formerly Communist country of Bulgaria, for instance, includes a version of the political guarantees found in the U.S. Bill of Rights, such as freedom from illegal search and detention, the right to a fair hearing at trial, and freedom of religion, expression, and association. But the document also goes much further, including such clauses that declare mothers "shall be guaranteed prenatal and postnatal leave, free obstetric care, alleviated working conditions, and other social assistance" and that workers "shall be entitled to healthy and nonhazardous working conditions to guaranteed minimum pay and remuneration for the actual work performed, and to rest and leave." Other constitutional guarantees include social security and welfare aid, the protection of the physically and mentally handicapped, affordable medical insurance, education, and a clean environment.

By contrast, it is impossible to point to the text of the U.S. Constitution as justification for social and economic protections, beyond perhaps the vague mention of promoting the "general welfare" in the

Preamble. This is due in part to the great age of the U.S. Constitution. It was created at a time when improving citizens' quality of life was not seen as a major goal of government and designed by wealthy elites who needed no such assistance. The absence of explicit social and economic protections is also rooted in a longer-term skepticism of big government in American political culture, a theme discussed in Chapter 11.

Today, of course, national, state, and local governments, as well as court rulings and bureaucratic decisions, have in fact enacted many of the types of social and economic protections described in other constitutions, such as minimum wage laws and environmental regulations. In fact, the United States actually delivers many of these protections more effectively, in practice, than countries that due to poverty, corruption, neglect, or other factors, do not live up to their loftily worded constitutions. Yet it remains the case that attempts by the government to improve the social and economic conditions of its citizenry remain among the most contested and controversial issues in American politics. Indeed, one of the major points of conflicts between liberals and conservatives throughout the twentieth century was over whether to expand or contract The New Deal, Franklin Delano Roosevelt's Depression-era plan for government intervention into the economy and the promotion of a safety net of government-run social programs.

This debate continues down to the current day, although in somewhat more muted form. In most democratic countries, an expansive role for the government in offering social welfare programs is well established and largely uncontroversial. But in the United States, a large swath of the American public, and in particular the American political class, remains opposed to such a role. Had the U.S. Constitution been textually altered to guarantee certain protections, the country would likely have moved further beyond these debates and more closely resemble other countries. But in the absence of such an authoritative statement, the issue of welfare payments was a potent political topic as recently as the 1990s, the scope of Social Security and Medicare remain very much active issues today, and the United States is the sole industrialized democracy to lack universal health care coverage for its citizens.

By contrast, the U.S. Constitution and the federal court system tasked with interpreting it offer a strident defense of the political rights both of individuals and of certain disadvantaged groups. The First Amendment's guarantee of freedom of expression is especially robust. The broad scope of protections for free speech, press, and peaceable assembly—all viewed as essential underpinnings for free society—are as close to absolute as any liberties or rights anywhere in the world. By contrast, the governments of many countries in the world to some degree control the content of their media, either formally under law or informally by extralegal pressure. China and Iran, for instance, impose stringent filters on the computer servers operating within their borders to prevent Internet users from accessing certain types of information, and also try to control access to television satellite dishes.

The U.S. government, however, lacks the power to limit the media; except in instances that might create an imminent threat to national security, Americans are free to air their views. (Those who knowingly publish falsehoods can be sued for libel by aggrieved parties after the fact, but elected officials and other public figures have relatively little protection under the law, given that the public has a stake in their activities.) Even highly unpopular forms of political expression have been repeatedly upheld by courts. Neo-Nazis and members of the Ku Klux Klan have the same right to march and demonstrate as others, and the burning of the U.S. flag has been ruled a legitimate means of political expression. By contrast, some democratic nations declare certain sensitive subjects out of bounds: for example, Germany prohibits denial of the Holocaust, Turkey has outlawed public acknowledgments of the early twentieth century Ottoman slaughter of Armenians, and France has outlawed denial of both events.

Other civil liberties also have a high degree of protection under the U.S. Constitution, sometimes in ways that are baffling to foreigners. One such liberty is the right to keep and bear arms under the Second Amendment, which thwarts attempts to control access to firearms. Although the founders may have been mostly concerned about maintaining viable state militias, individual gun ownership is an established liberty in the United States. Americans also have a far-reaching right to freely express their religious views, but at the same time the strict separation of church and state has been vigorously enforced by courts in recent decades. By contrast, in many countries, certain religious traditions, such as Roman Catholicism in Latin America and Islam in Arab countries, enjoy a special status, which may curb the rights of those who adhere to nonmajority religions. The U.S. Constitution also provided strict procedures for due process of law, to the extent that evidence gathered by police in violation of the Fourth Amendment protection against "unreasonable search and seizure" can be excluded from court proceedings. Under this exclusionary rule, many individuals have been acquitted of crimes who might well be judged guilty in court systems more concerned with maintaining social control than safeguarding individual rights.

Conclusion

More than 215 years after its enactment, the U.S. Constitution remains partly a global prototype and partly an anachronistic anomaly. Constitutions are important in all countries, but because of its great longevity and the enormous reverence with which it is treated, the U.S. Constitution is even more central to American political life, even political identity, than almost any other such document in the world. Presidents swear to "preserve, protect and defend the constitution" in their oath of office, naturalizing citizens are required to uphold the constitution, and school children routinely pledge allegiance to the republic created by the Constitution. Understanding its form, content, and idiosyncracies is an essential first step in understanding the country itself.

Further Reading

- *Comparative Constitutional Engineering: An Inquiry into Structures, Incentives and Outcomes.* Giovanni Sartori. New York University Press, New York: 1997.
- *Constitutions of the World.* Robert L. Maddex. CQ Press, Washington, DC: 1995.

- *How Democratic is the American Constitution?* Robert A. Dahl. Yale University Press, New Haven, CT: 2002.

Web-Based Exploration Exercise

Find and read through the constitutions of any two countries of the world other than the United States; ideally, you should choose one democratic country and one nondemocratic country. Then compare them with the U.S. Constitution. Identify and report back on two significant similarities and two significant differences that you found among the three documents. A comprehensive portal to constitutions of the world, many but not all in English, can be found at <www.findlaw.com/01topics/06constitutional/03forconst/index.html>

Question for Debate and Discussion

The U.S. Constitution includes a provision by which it could be replaced: the Constitutional Convention. Because this has never occurred in U.S. history, it is unclear what exactly would transpire at such a convention and what its limitations might be, if any. Critics note that the first Constitutional Convention completely eliminated the existing system, the Articles of Confederation. What advantages might there be to starting with a clean slate in the United States? Could these outweigh the dangers and disadvantages? What sweeping changes might be desirable? Could these changes be more effectively enacted through the more common procedure of the amendment process?

3

FEDERALISM

Virtually all countries have two levels of government in common. *National-level* government generally deals with foreign affairs, defense, managing currency, and the regulation of commerce, although often much more. *Local-level* government tends to focus on more mundane and smaller-scale issues, managing day-to-day concerns in areas such as police departments, sanitation, and land-use zoning. Where countries differ significantly is between the national and the local governments, at the level most commonly termed provinces, but also known by such terms as departments, states, cantons, or prefectures.

Three principal models exist to describe the interrelationship between governments at the national and provincial levels. *Confederations* or *confederal states* are those in which there exists an identifiable national-level government but in which most or all final decision making remains vested at the provincial level. By contrast, in *unitary states*, governing authority is clearly concentrated at the national level, with all or most important decisions made in the capital city and then merely delegated for enactment and administration at the provincial level. The third model, that of the *federation* or *federal state*, strikes a middle path between confederal and unitary approaches, with decision-making authority carefully divided between and shared by the national and provincial levels. The United States is an example of a robust federal system, in which the fifty states of the union (the provincial level of government in the United States) have distinct areas of authority within which the national government may not freely encroach or interfere.

Case Study: Confederation in Bosnia

One tragic chapter in the collapse of Communism in Europe was the disintegration of the multiethnic country of Yugoslavia, which culminated in a brutal war in the central region of Bosnia where armed conflict and acts of genocide led to a quarter of a million deaths between 1992 and 1995. Under international pressure, the three major Bosnian ethnic groups—Muslims, Serbs, and Croats—negotiated a peace agreement in Dayton, Ohio. Given international concern that Yugoslavia might fragment into ever-smaller, warring factions, one provision of the Dayton Peace Agreement was that Bosnia be maintained as a single country. But how could the three deeply embittered ethnic groups find a way to coexist in a single state? The solution was to design a complex new political architecture that the peace accords termed a federation but which was, in theory and especially in practice, really a confederation. Thus the new Bosnian government would consist of two powerful regional entities, one for Serbs and a second for Muslims and Croats together. Although this would suggest a two-part structure, in fact the Muslim–Croat section itself had distinct subgovernments for each group.

This extremely decentralized, three-part system was reflected in the existence of a three-member collective presidency at the national level and the establishment of political, fiscal, and administrative autonomy within each group. The central government was tasked with conducting most aspects of foreign and trade policy, managing currency and finances, and coordinating some aspects of relations between the three groups. But the three entities managed almost all other aspects of governance, had the sole authority to tax, could exercise a veto over most national legislation, and even maintained their own armies under only nominal national control. In practice, they paid relatively little attention to the national government and rarely cooperated among themselves.

In 2005, a series of reappraisals were conducted on the tenth anniversary of the Dayton Peace Agreement. While the crucial goal of ending bloodshed had been achieved by the accord, it was almost universally acknowledged that the country was held together mainly by the presence of international peacekeeping troops and administrators empowered to impose solutions when the groups came to an impasse. The confederal system had obscured lines of responsibility, made governmental accountability all but impossible, and promoted corruption and economic stagnation—all while doing little to create a viable country. The status quo was recognized as, at best, a stop-gap solution, and partition into separate countries, or unification with adjacent areas of Croatia and Serbia, seemed as likely a prospect as ever.

The Confederal Model: Many Weaknesses, Few Strengths

Although far from a confederal system today, the first, short-lived regime in the United States was not that of the Constitution but the Articles of Confederation. In 1781, in the immediate aftermath of the American Revolution, the thirteen states recognized their need to coordinate among themselves but still jealously guarded their newfound freedom and independence. They thus enacted the Articles of Confederation, which created an extremely weak national government with no president or other national executive leadership, no power to tax or to regulate interstate commerce, and no power to act on major issues without the unanimous consent of the states. This led to an eight-year period of ruinous instability, with the national government unable to carry out even basic functions, the states engaging in economic conflict that threatened to turn into actual warfare, and each state wielding an effective veto over the national government. It was in specific response to the weaknesses of the Articles of Confederation that the Constitution was enacted in 1789 "in order to form a more perfect union" and to serve as the "supreme law of the land," creating strong national-level government and turning the United States into a federation.

The idea of confederation would not disappear in American history, resurfacing during the U.S. Civil War under the banner of states' rights. Although the Confederate States of America never had the opportunity to govern outside of wartime, there is little reason to believe that its decentralized structure would have proven effective. Some historians have, in fact, argued that the power that each Confederate governor had over the deployment of the troops from their state hindered the development of a coherent national defense strategy and contributed to the military defeat of the South. Overall, the American experience with confederation has not been anomalous, but rather a prototypical example of the need for reasonably strong national-level government.

Reviewing the world today, it is difficult to find an example of a true confederation. Switzerland was a confederation for over 500 years, and today remains the functioning state with perhaps the greatest devolution of power to its provinces (called "cantons"); still it is regarded as a federation because its national government does retain some key areas of distinct authority. The term used for the founding of Canada was *confederation*, but it is nonetheless now better described as a fairly decentralized federation, with a great deal of authority exercised both in Ottawa and in the ten provincial capitals. The European Union (EU) today, although not a state, perhaps most closely reflects some of the key characteristics of a confederation, with sovereign power retained by member countries that voluntarily cede significant decision-making authority to the EU capital in Brussels. Despite their high degree of economic coordination, the EU national governments retain far greater latitude than the provinces of any country could maintain. Indeed, the EU has found it difficult to coordinate its foreign and military policies, underscoring the limitations of the confederal model.

It may be that the best use of the confederal model in the world today is the one seen in Bosnia, namely as a transitional device when a stronger national government is not politically feasible (much as was the case in the United States in 1781). Developments elsewhere in the former Yugoslavia suggest that confederation might also be used as a transitional phase to independence. The last two remaining parts of the former Yugoslavia to still be formally linked, the Union of Serbia and Montenegro, gradually moved from a federal toward a confederal model and finally to complete independence in 2006. As of this writing, a confederation seems to be the best hope for maintaining a single Iraqi state but this might, as in the Yugoslav example, prove to be only a way station toward the creation of separate Sunni, Shiite, and Kurdish states.

Case Study: The Unitary State in Japan

One of the major political tasks facing the United States and its allies at the end of World War II was to construct new modes of governance in the defeated states of Germany and Japan that would help to prevent future aggression on their part. Both political systems had become deeply dysfunctional in the prewar period, Japan under the influence of an expansionist military, Germany under the control of the Nazi party. Part of the solution was a long-term military occupation, but part of it was to create new constitutional norms that promoted democracy and decentralized power. With regards to federalism, however, the two states ended up with radically different systems, Japan emerging as a classic unitary state, Germany a robust federal republic.

In 1945, Germany was a nation located in the middle of a continent and had been unified into a single state for less than a century. But Japan was an isolated island nation claiming more than 2,500 years of unbroken continuity from the first Emperor and the founding of the early Japanese state. The U.S.-imposed Constitution of 1946 focused its attention on the elimination of the political role of the Emperor, reducing him to a powerless "symbol of the state," but it could not overcome the legacy of centuries of centralized rule. Democratization was achieved by strictly limiting the role of the military and promoting a parliamentary democracy, but virtually all decision-making authority remained vested in politicians and, particularly, in bureaucrats located in Tokyo.

Today, Japan has forty-seven prefectures (or provinces) and although each has its own elected government, their roles are largely administrative. Tokyo defines political structures and laws that are binding on the prefectures (and also on the country's many municipalities below the prefecture level). Municipal and prefecture governments may be delegated the task of figuring out how best to apply a centrally made decision, such as in the construction of schools or the organization of hospital systems. But rulings handed down by the national government always take precedence over prefectures, and there are numerous topics with which the prefectures cannot become involved. Further, they rely on subsidies from the central government rather than having their own power to levy taxes. In short, prefectures are used by the central government when convenient, disregarded when not.

Unitary States: Centralized Decision Making

The most common form of government in the world is that of the unitary state in which final decision-making authority rests squarely at the national level. To be sure, provincial governments may exist in unitary states, but they are created by the central governments for their own convenience and may be directed and overridden more or less at will. Before the American Revolution, the thirteen colonies were subject to the unitary authority of the British king, who appointed and directed the work of powerful colonial governors. Such strong central government was the norm not only in the American colonies, but also among many monarchies in which centralized power had been concentrated in the hands of a single sovereign. Indeed, one of the major breakthroughs of American constitutional theory was the idea that sovereignty could be divisible, *shared* at both the national and state governments. This was possible because the ultimate source of the authority of both national and state government was the people themselves, hence the new concept of popular sovereignty.

Today, the unitary model of government remains the most common form of government in the world, used by nearly seven-eighths of the world's national governments. Among nondemocratic states, it is in practice the norm for all final decision-making authority to reside with the executive branch of the national government. Thus, centralized decision making and almost exclusively top-down lines of authority can be found in most nondemocratic countries, such as China, in which the Beijing-based Communist government can and routinely does direct the affairs of the entire country, and Saudi Arabia, where the royal family dictates public policy. Even some nondemocratic countries that are nominally federations, such as Pakistan, may in practice operate as unitary states, at least during frequent periods of military or other dictatorship.

Although the unitary model is closely associated with nondemocratic systems, many democracies are also unitary states. The unitary model is particularly well suited to small countries in which it is relatively easy for the entire country to be administered from the capital city. But there are also a number of larger states that are unitary states. In addition to the example of Japan, another well-known unitary state is France, where various departments are established almost entirely for the convenience of the national government, to which they are wholly subordinate. So entrenched is the sense of France as a single, indivisible whole that even some overseas departments, such as Reunion Island in the South Pacific and French Guiana in South America, are formally considered to be as integral a part of France as Normandy or the Loire Valley. Recent discussion of giving quasi-autonomy to the island of Corsica in order to quell nationalist fervor there was rejected as compromising the unitary character of the state. However, not all unitary states are as rigid as France (and even France does have active local governments). Great Britain is a unitary state but since 1997 has undertaken significant devolution of power, creating new regional parliaments in Scotland, Wales, and Northern Ireland, and strengthening self-governance in the City of London.

In the United States, the unitary model is an alien idea at the national level. The fifty state governments emphatically exercise power in many areas in their own right, without its having been granted by or devolved from Washington. Notably, however, the *internal* political organization of U.S. states follows a unitary model. Whereas the states of the Union preceded the national government and are in some regards equal to it, the thousands of city and county governments established *within* states are wholly creations of those state governments. In practice, cities may exercise a great deal of home rule and, based on their large populations, may be quite influential in the politics of their states and even the country. Still, even entities as sprawling and complex as Los Angeles or Chicago are mere expressions of the will of the states of California or Illinois, which retain final authority over their cities. Constitutionally there is nothing to keep the state government from managing almost all aspects of governance throughout the state. (One major exception to the unitary aspects of state government is the territories held by Native American tribes, which have direct relations with the U.S. government and bypass state authority.)

Case Study: German Federalism

Even a casual tourist to Germany can discern that the unified country is a relatively recent political construction with multiple historical power centers ranging from Berlin to Munich to Hamburg to Frankfort to Cologne. Unlike long-established unitary states such as France and Great Britain, which are utterly dominated by Paris and London, respectively, the diversity of major cities in Germany reflects the reality that the country was unified only in 1871. In seeking to dismantle the highly centralized Nazi regime after World War II and deter renewed military aggression then, the Allied Powers tapped into this history by creating a new Federal Republic of Germany, commonly called West Germany during the Cold War to distinguish it from Communist-controlled East Germany.

The Allies' imposition of federalism, along with other measures, worked extraordinarily well: postwar West Germany became a model democratic, even pacifist, country with powerful provinces called Länder. So strong was the force of history and these new constitutional arrangements that after the collapse of Communism, East Germany abolished itself as a country and reorganized into separate Länder, each of which was then individually unified into the Federal Republic of Germany.

Today, the sixteen Länder continue to enjoy an exceptional degree of influence, all part of the enduring plan to prevent a return to tyranny in Germany. Indeed, the central government has relatively few powers entirely to itself, mostly relating to military, border, and diplomatic issues. Some powers are reserved to the Länder, such as those pertaining to police, public order, and education, but most areas of legislation are subject to the concurrent jurisdiction of both. Similarly, the power to tax and allocate revenues is exercised by both the federal and Länder governments.

The German system even goes so far as to give the leaders of the Länder the ability to directly influence federal lawmaking. Members of the upper house of parliament, the Bundesrat, are essentially ambassadors from the governments of the Länder, not elected by the people but appointed by the governors of the Länder and subject to their direction. The upper house has a veto over any issues falling under concurrent jurisdiction and can even block any legislation relating to federal jurisdiction unless overridden by 60 percent of the lower house. This direct influence of the Länder on national politics is exceptional, so in this regard German federalism represents an unusually strong system of checks on national authorities.

The Federal Model: Unity in Diversity

Only about twenty-five countries, just over one-eighth the world's total, have federal political systems. But because federal systems are particularly well suited to diverse, populous countries, these twenty-five countries represent some 40 percent of the world's population, most notably India, Brazil, Germany, Mexico, Nigeria, Russia, and the United States. Federalism is also well suited to sparsely populated states with large territories to govern, such as the largely underpopulated landmasses of Canada, Australia, and Argentina. Even in relatively small countries, federalism can be helpful when the population is deeply divided along ethnic, religious, linguistic, or other lines, as in Belgium and Switzerland. (The other officially established federations in the world are Austria, Bosnia, Comoros, Ethiopia, Iraq, Malaysia, Micronesia, St. Kitts and Nevis, Sudan, the United Arab Emirates, and Venezuela; all others are formally unitary states.)

The advantages of federalism are manifold. Simply put, the larger and more diverse the territory and population of a country, the harder it is to find "one size fits all" solutions. This challenge is all the greater in democratic systems, in which government must demonstrate high degrees of responsiveness to the wishes of the people. The relatively few populous countries that do not employ a federal system are either undemocratic, such as China, or largely homogenous in population, such as Japan. The large, populous, and diverse country of Indonesia has long rejected federalism, a decision that has contributed to numerous armed insurrections and ongoing civil strife ranging from one end of the country at Aceh to the other at East Timor, which won independence in 2002.

The relevant political science concept here is that of *subsidiarity*, or the idea that as many decisions as possible should be made as close as possible to the people. Hence, the state government in Bismarck, North Dakota, is seen as better able to decide on the distribution of public health resources within its thinly populated state than a model designed in Washington, which might be weighted toward states with larger and denser populations. The same basic logic of subsidiarity also helps lead the state of North Dakota to provide its largest cities, such as Fargo and Grand Forks, with local latitude to run their own health departments geared toward those more urban settings.

This distribution of authority can help to tailor programs and maximize the effectiveness of services. It also relieves the burden from national government of managing such a huge array of varied concerns, allowing it to focus on its own major responsibilities, such as foreign policy and national defense. A federal system also allows for flexibility and innovation, from which the entire system may benefit. This led U.S. Supreme Court Justice Louis Brandeis to call the states "laboratories of democracy" in which different approaches to governance and public policy can be tried out and evaluated for their effectiveness. True federalism, however, involves more than merely operational latitude in implementing priorities set at the national level. In this regard, federal systems fall along a spectrum, with some provincial-level leaders clearly able to refuse or resist orders from the national leadership while others can only protest or perhaps delay such orders. The governors of U.S. states or the premiers of Canadian provinces would fall at the stronger end of that spectrum, their counterparts in Mexico and India at the weaker end.

Despite the generally democracy-promoting aspects of federalism, there are also some troublesome features. One major concern arises when areas of responsibility become too intertwined. The educational system in the United States, for example, has sometimes been criticized as being directed at too many levels, with different agencies that operate in competing or even conflicting ways at the national, state, county, and local levels. American students lag behind their counterparts in many other countries, and rates of functional illiteracy are strikingly high among some segments of the population. Similarly, health programs are jointly and awkwardly funded and administered by multiple levels of government. The United States spends far more than other countries on health care yet has produced troubling results in areas such as preventive medicine and maternal health care. Shortcomings in areas such as education and health care are not necessarily *caused* by federalism, but may be exacerbated and prolonged by the decentralization and lack of coordination that federalism can bring.

In times of crisis, tangled lines of authority can also lead to problems, such as when the national government, the Louisiana state government, and the New Orleans city government failed to properly coordinate their efforts during the 2005 Hurricane Katrina crisis. Partly as a result of this failure, neither city emergency services nor the state National Guard nor the Federal Emergency Management Agency were able to effectively evacuate the city or come to the aid of the survivors. On the other hand, the response to the September 11, 2001, terrorist attacks in New York City highlighted some of the flexibility and adaptability of a federal system, with national, state, and local governments each responding in a coordinated fashion within the respective spheres of their expertise and responsibility. Within an hour of the attacks, the city police and fire forces took command of "Ground Zero," the state mobilized health care resources, and the U.S. Air Force secured the city's airspace.

Beyond problems of coordination, there are also serious dangers in federalism that have gone too far, or in which the balance of power between the national and provincial government is unclear or unstable. Indeed, the great Constitutional failure in the American experience, the catastrophic American Civil War, was directly rooted in differing interpretations of states' rights. Although resolved by bloodshed in the 1860s, many of the same issues resurfaced in the 1950s and 1960s during the Civil Rights Movement, when the national government finally moved to protect its African-American citizens from state-level segregation policies. (It should be noted that while American regional identities, particularly that of the South, may have a significant de facto influence on politics, such regions have no distinctive constitutional status. This is a typical feature of federal systems worldwide, in which there are rarely regional governments established between the national and provincial level.)

The form of federalism in different countries is also greatly shaped by why the federal model is in use in the first place. Some countries at the time of their founding were created out of preexisting entities, as was the case in the United States and Canada. In such cases, federalism may be the price of national unification; states or provinces may be unwilling to accede to a strong national union unless they are guaranteed a significant continuing role. In other democracies, federalist principles can be introduced into a previously unitary state to dampen separatist impulses among ethnic minorities. Spain, for instance, has increasingly reinterpreted its constitution to allow greater and greater regional autonomy in the far north, hoping that this will deter separationist impulses among ethnically and linguistically distinctive Basques and Catalans.

Conclusion

The United States was the first federal country, and has been an enormous influence on the subsequent development of federalism throughout the world. Despite some failings, federalism has, on the whole, served the geographically vast and demographically diverse country well. But federalism today remains a system employed by only a minority of countries in the world, and in the United States, the states of the Union remain essentially unitary in their operation. Confederation, on the other hand, is a largely failed model that the United States was wise to put behind it with the passage of the Constitution of 1789.

Further Reading

- *Constitutional Origins, Structure, and Change in Federal Countries.* John Kincaid and G. Alan Tarr, Eds. Published for the Forum of Federations and the International Association of Centers for International Studies, McGill-Queen's University

Press, Montreal, Quebec, and Kingston, Ontario, Canada: 1996.

- *Handbook of Federal Countries.* Ann L. Griffiths, Ed. Published for the Forum of Federations and the International Association of Centers for International Studies, McGill-Queen's University Press, Montreal, Quebec, and Kingston, Ontario, Canada: 2002.
- *Comparing Federal Systems in the 1990s.* Ronald Watts. Institute of Intergovernmental Relations, Queen's University, Kingston, Ontario, Canada: 1996.

Web-Based Exploration Exercise

Visit the Web site for the government of any state in the United States. (The Web site of any state can be reached at <www.state.XX.us> by substituting the state's two-letter postal code in place of the XX; for instance New York State can be reached at <www.state.ny.gov>). Then visit the Web sites for one of the provinces or states of another country; a useful listing can be found at <www.forumfed.org/federalism/cntrylist.asp?lang=en>. Identify and explain any two similarities and two differences between the governmental structure and activities of a U.S. state and those of the other province or state you explored.

Question for Debate and Discussion

As a federal country, the United States has a complex and multilayered system of government. What advantages would you see to reorganizing political power in the United States to be more along the lines of a unitary state? What might be lost if the United States were to do so? Can you see any arguments for moving toward a more confederal model?

4

SEPARATION OF POWERS

The most distinctive of all the institutional arrangements of the U.S. government is its strict separation of powers into clearly divided executive, legislative, and judicial branches. This separation of powers is in many ways the cornerstone of the U.S. Constitutional edifice, and according to the founders, democracy is virtually impossible without such a separation of powers. As James Madison wrote in *Federalist 47*, "The accumulation of powers, legislative, executive, and judiciary ... may justly be pronounced the very definition of tyranny."

The separation of powers established in the U.S. Constitution has several different dimensions. First is the institutional separation of the president from Congress and of both these political branches from the federal court system. Because no one can simultaneously hold a position in more than one branch, senators or U.S. representatives who wish to become cabinet secretaries must leave Congress to do so, and members of Congress must resign before becoming president or vice president (although the vice president does ceremonially preside over the Senate). Federal judges, likewise, cannot hold legislative or executive positions, and no one can hold state and federal office simultaneously.

Separation of powers is further re-enforced by the president, senators, and representatives having different terms of office (four, six, and two years, respectively) and different constituencies (the entire country, states, and congressional districts, respectively.) Federal judges, meanwhile, have lifetime tenure, and their only constituency is the U.S. Constitution itself. Finally, the goal of preventing tyranny is further advanced by the system of checks and balances, most notably the presidential veto, the congressional impeachment authority, the senate's power to advise and consent to presidential appointments, and the Supreme Court's power of judicial review of executive and legislative acts.

Given this emphasis on "ambition countering ambition" as Madison called it, many Americans are surprised to learn that the strict separation of powers (especially of executive and legislative powers) is a rarity among established democracies. In fact, the United States is the *only* advanced industrialized democracy to have a full separation-of-powers system in which a powerful president must contend with a powerful, separately elected Congress and an independent judiciary with final say on constitutional issues. Further, there seems to be little desire for newly emerging nations to adopt an American-style strict separation of powers system. Even in Iraq, where the United States had a major role in establishing the new governmental structure after the overthrow of Saddam Hussein, a separation-of-powers system was rejected. Indeed, the separation of powers may be regarded as perhaps the greatest American anomaly of all.

The system encouraged in Iraq, and employed in most democratic, industrialized nations, is the *parliamentary system*. Many Americans are aware that most other democratic countries call their national legislatures not a congress but a parliament, and that the chief leader is not a president but a prime minister. But there may also be a tendency to think that these are simply differences in terminology rather than substance and that the two systems function in largely the same way. In fact, however, the two types of governmental arrangements are not simply different, but in some ways are polar opposites. The single most crucial difference is that in a parliamentary system, executive authority *arises out of* control of the legislature. Whereas one cannot hold a seat in Congress and be president at the same time in the U.S. system, one generally must be both a member of and the uncontested leader of the lower house of the legislature in order to be prime minister. This fusion of legislative and executive authority means that the goal of a parliamentary system is the *concentration* of power, while the U.S. separation-of-powers system (also called a "presidential system") is specifically designed to achieve the opposite result of a *dispersal* of power. Whereas a measure of inefficiency is deliberately built into the U.S. system as a way of countering tyranny, streamlined efficiency is the key attribute of most parliamentary systems.

Case Study: The Westminster Parliamentary Model

Although they all bear certain key characteristics, parliamentary systems vary widely in their specifics. But the prototype for all such systems is that found in Great Britain, which is regarded as the "Mother of Parliaments" and source of the "Westminster Model," a name derived from the area of London in which it is located. The British parliamentary system is considered particularly important for two primary reasons. First, it was the earliest such system to develop and the longest to be in continuous operation. Second, most other parliaments are to some extent based on the British precedent. In the case of many countries of the former British Empire, such as India, Jamaica, Canada, Australia, and New Zealand, the Westminster model was explicitly imported (although always with some local modifications). Parliaments found in many other countries, particularly in Western Europe, contain stronger homegrown elements but are nonetheless to one degree or another similar to the Westminster Model.

Unlike most other modern systems, the British parliament evolved over the course of many centuries, shifting, adapting, and accruing various idiosyncrasies along the way and never being codified into a single written constitution. Today, sovereign power—or the right to govern—is said to emanate from "The Crown in Parliament." The Crown, or the monarchy, remains a hereditary office invested in one person from the time of accession to natural death; the current queen, Elizabeth II, has held that title since the death of her father in 1952. The Parliament is composed of two separate chambers, the House of Lords and the House of Commons, working in conjunction with the monarch.

Until the late 1990s, most of the members of the House of Lords were noblemen (along with a few women) who inherited titles such as duke, marquess, earl, viscount, and baron upon the death of their fathers (or, occasionally, other close relatives) and served for the rest of their lives. However, beginning in 1958, there also began the practice of granting "life peerages" to accomplished individuals in British society, entitling them (although not their descendants) to the title of lord or lady and to a seat in the

House of Lords until their deaths. Others with seats in the House of Lords include the bishops of the Church of England (called the "Lords Spiritual") and the "Law Lords" who meet separately to hear legal cases as the final and highest court of appeal in the judicial branch in Great Britain.

Early in British history, most political power was wielded by the monarch, who claimed a right to rule based on divine mandate as well as military power. The growing power of land-based British nobles forced a power-sharing arrangement, as enshrined in the Magna Carta of 1215, leading eventually to the founding of a House of Lords in London to serve as a voice for the interests of the nobles. While British monarchs remained politically potent, they began to choose a principal officer, called a prime minister, from out of the House of Lords to manage the affairs of government. As power began to shift from the countryside to the cities, another, initially less powerful chamber, was added to Parliament called the House of "Commons" to note that it reflected the interests of people who were neither royalty nor nobility. Indeed, it is still referred to as the lower house of parliament, a term used in many other countries to describe the house that is in some electoral sense closest to the people. Throughout the nineteenth century, more and more of the authority that was once wielded by the monarchy in concert with the nobility was slowly transferred to the Commons, and in particular to the prime minister that it elects and the cabinet of ministers that are appointed by the prime minister. By the mid-1800s, British political journalist Walter Bagehot famously described the monarch and the House of Lords as the "dignified" rather than the "efficient" parts of government, representing tradition rather than day-to-day governance.

Today, the House of Commons has the final say on all legislative matters and yields all executive authority. The British monarch performs only ceremonial functions, acting as the country's formal head of state by embodying the historical continuity and national unity of the country while staying entirely out of politics and above partisanship. The executive power once wielded by monarchs is now vested in a cabinet of government ministers led by a prime minister, all drawn from among the members of parliament. The basis for their exercise of executive authority resides not in selection by the monarch but from support of a majority in the House of Commons. Meanwhile, the House of Lords has been reduced to an essentially consultative role and remains a body very much in transition, with most of the hereditary lords removed from office and other changes under consideration.

The Fusion of Power in Parliamentary Government

As the case study above describes, it is possible to talk about distinctive forms of executive, legislative, and judicial power in the British parliamentary system. What is not possible is to neatly disentangle them into separate institutions and spheres of influence. (No office in Britain reflects this more clearly than that of the Lord Chancellor, who has traditionally been Speaker of the House of Lords, the head of the highest court, *and* a member of the executive cabinet!) In parliamentary systems, executive, legislative, and (to a considerably lesser extent) judicial powers overlap and intersect in a variety of ways that are quite distinct from the U.S. system, with significant results for the functioning of those governments. Below is an overview of the ways in which power is concentrated rather than separated in parliamentary systems, based largely on the Westminster Model.

Under the separation of powers system, the U.S. president serves as both the symbolic head of state and hands-on head of government. As seen in the case study of Great Britain, however, parliamentary systems employ a dual executive system in which the loftier ceremonial duties of office are separated off from the partisan and political work of making policy and running a government. In parliamentary systems, the role of ceremonial head of state is played by either hereditary monarchs, such as the King of Spain, or figurehead presidents, such as the President of Germany, who lend their dignity to proceedings of state, such as the opening of parliament, but who wield little or no actual executive authority. These heads of state, then, generally play no role in the separation of powers scheme precisely because they do not wield any real power. (A few countries, notably France and Russia, have so-called semipresidential systems in which the head of state does exercise real power. The head of state role is discussed in more detail in Chapter 5).

To find the institution where power is actually exercised in a parliament, it is necessary to look to the lower house of the legislature and in particular to its leader, the prime minister (an office sometimes also called a premier or a chancellor). In democratic systems, these lower houses are invariably elected directly by the people and, thus, draw their claim to rule from the consent of the governed. Control of a majority of seats in the parliament, then, is equated with the support of a majority of the population—the ultimate form of democratic legitimacy. At the start of each new parliament, a prime minister is selected based upon his or her ability to garner the support of more than half the members of the chamber. Because they must have worked their way to the top of a major political party, prime ministers are usually well known, long-established politicians on the national stage, perhaps even household names in their countries. (The American experience of electing "Washington outsiders"—often little-known state governors such as Bill Clinton of Arkansas—to the presidency is quite alien to parliamentary systems.)

In countries with only two main political parties, the prime minister will generally be the leader of the party that holds an outright majority of seats. In countries with multiple political parties, the picture can be somewhat more complicated when no single party holds an outright majority. In this case, negotiations may be necessary to form a coalition of parties that collectively control a majority of seats; ordinarily, the leader of the party with the largest number of seats will become the prime minister. Sometimes, the choice of a coalition partner is clear, and one or more small parties will join the larger party, usually in exchange for control of a key ministry or area of policy. Thus, for instance, a small rural-based party might join a coalition in exchange for control of the agriculture ministry. As might be expected, the more numerous and diverse the coalition partners, the harder it becomes for a prime minister to assemble a stable coalition. Thus, coalitions tend to expand only to the point needed to ensure the support of more than half the members of the lower house.

In relatively unusual cases, however, two large parties who are ordinarily political rivals may agree to join as more or less equals in a "grand coalition." This occurs mainly when neither of the large parties can find a coalition partner to form a majority on their own, and they believe that a quick new election will be equally inconclusive. Such a grand coalition was struck after the 2005 elections in Germany between the center-right Christian Democrats and the center-left Social Democrats. Another possible arrangement occurs when a party that falls a bit short of an outright majority is allowed by the opposition parties to operate as a "minority government," negotiating issues on a one-by-one basis. After Canadian elections in 2006, the Conservative Party won only 125 out of 308 seats but was permitted by the opposition parties to cautiously govern under Prime Minister Stephen Harper.

Whatever the specific circumstances, the prime minister will next appoint a cabinet of ministers to compose the new government. This government will exercise executive powers for as long as it maintains a parliamentary majority, or until the maximum time elapses before the law requires a new election to be called (a period usually of about four or five years). At any time during the life of a parliament, many systems allow the prime minister to call for a new election. This will often come at a time when only a year or so is left before elections must be called, and the prime minister perceives some political advantage for calling an early election, such as when his or her party is particularly popular or when political opponents are in disarray. Thus, parliamentary terms of office can vary widely and unpredictably, and national elections can be scheduled with just a few weeks' notice. This is a marked contrast to the American system, where both executive and legislative terms of office are highly fixed and inflexible—presidential and congressional elections in the United States have been held on a rigid schedule, without interruption, since 1789. Members of parliament are also all elected on the same day and will serve for the same amount of time, another distinction from the deliberately staggered election dates and terms of office for U.S. representatives, senators, and the president.

One of the first tasks of a new prime minister is to appoint other ministers to run portfolios including foreign affairs, defense, finance, justice, the environment, and many other areas. Like the prime minister, these ministers generally must be members of parliament, and together they compose a cabinet that shares collective responsibility for the actions of the government. Formally, the prime minister is regarded as just another member of parliament, and as a "first among equals" within the cabinet. Not being directly elected by the people, the prime minister—unlike an American president—claims no independent mandate to govern and is accountable to parliament as a whole (although *not* to the cabinet), which can remove him or her at any time. In practice, however, voters in parliamentary systems often know—and have their choice of party influenced by—who will be prime minister when they cast their votes, which can give a prime minister a greater personal mandate. Further, while a parliament can remove a prime minister from office, this is usually much easier said than done as will be discussed further below. Indeed, while they enjoy a solid parliamentary majority, prime ministers often wield extensive powers that are largely unchecked by other political actors and institutions.

Prime Ministerial Power

Prime ministers are so formidably powerful precisely because they not only lead the executive but also exert control over their majority in the lower house, ensuring that they usually can pass any legislation they choose. It may not be easy to maneuver oneself to become the prime minister, but once in office he or she has an array of institutional prerogatives. In addition to appointing ministers, he or she can usually dismiss them or reassign them, making members of the cabinet unable or unwilling to publicly challenge the prime minister, at least not in public once a decision has been taken. Cabinet ministers are ordinarily required to support the official position of government on all matters, on threat of dismissal and even expulsion from the party. About the most that a cabinet member can do is resign on principle, perhaps briefly embarrassing the prime minister. While cabinet ministers often do have a good deal of autonomy within their departments and can certainly bring pressure to bear on the decisions of government, they cannot hope to prevail in direct conflict with a prime minister.

The prime minister also has tremendous control over the rank-and-file members of his or her party who are in parliament (often called "backbenchers" because of where they are seated in the chamber). Ideally, the relationship between backbenchers and their leaders should be one of cooperation and mutual support, with leaders carefully soliciting and heeding the wishes of their backbenchers. And while this is often the case, in times of conflict or dissention, prime ministers have formidable means by which to exert party discipline to ensure that backbenchers vote as their party leaders wish them to. In the United States, members of the Senate and House of Representatives can and do vote against their party leaders in Congress, often with little lasting consequence to themselves or to the leaders. But in parliaments, party leaders have the means to destroy the careers of backbenchers of their own party who challenge or oppose them. Party leaders are highly influential in the selection of their party nominees for office because most parliamentary systems do not have primary campaigns in which nominees are selected by the voters. Thus, party leaders can often deny renomination in the next election to members of parliament who do not vote as the party wishes. Party leaders also control who will be promoted out of the back benches to a junior ministerial position, then to a full ministerial position with a minor portfolio, and then to a top ministerial position. Displeasing the party leadership can, thus, be the equivalent of career suicide.

As might be expected, prime ministers whose majority is based on a coalition are often in a weaker position and must work more actively to allay the concerns of their coalition partners—particularly any party whose defection from the coalition would cause the loss of a parliamentary majority. In this case, prime ministers must negotiate with the heads of other parties, who in turn are expected to keep their own backbenchers in line. As will be seen, coalition partners and even the prime minister's own party do have the final say over the fate of a prime minister, so prime ministers have multiple incentives to keep their coalition partners and their own party backbenchers relatively contented and cooperative. But during ordinary times, they also have a much broader array of threats and inducements to ensure the support of their legislative majority than do Congressional leaders, and certainly more than do U.S. presidents, who have no direct power over members of Congress.

Finally, prime ministers are also able to largely ignore the members of parliament who are not from their party or coalition of parties. Such individuals are even less powerful than backbenchers in the majority. Their major role is to form the opposition, which has the right to challenge, question, and berate the government, use the media to air their grievances, and propose alternative programs to the public. The leader of the largest party outside of government may even take the title "Leader of the Opposition" and appoint a shadow cabinet paralleling the existing cabinet to serve as a government-in-waiting prepared to assume control of government on short notice. But for as long as they are outside of government, the opposition shares in no executive and quite little legislative power.

Other Checks and Balances?

Thus far, we have seen that prime ministers are mostly unchecked in their executive authority by either the formal head of state (who plays a symbolic role) or by the members of their own cabinet (who are subject to prime ministerial control). Likewise, we have seen that prime ministers are rarely limited in their legislative power by either the backbenchers of their own parties or the opposition in the lower house. Are there, then, other potential checks and balances on prime ministers that serve to reign them in?

One possibility would be the upper house of parliament in those very frequent cases where such an upper house exists. Depending upon the particular system, the upper house may at times be able to frustrate the goals of the prime minister. However, the case of the British House of Lords is not atypical in that formal or informal procedures often constrict the types of issues that the upper house can influence, particularly when they are revenue-related bills. Likewise, there are often formal and informal means by which lower houses can override the upper houses in the case of conflict. (The role of upper houses varies greatly and will be discussed in more detail in Chapter 6.) Broadly speaking, some upper houses can sometimes act as a check on prime ministers, but only in the legislative arena; they generally play little or no role in executive decisions.

Another possibility for checks and balances would be the judicial branch, and here again systems vary widely. There are some countries in which national supreme courts have the final say on issues relating to constitutional questions, and may have the ability to check the prime minister in some cases. By their very natures, however, many unelected judiciaries tend to avoid so-called political questions that they deem better left to the elected branches of government. Some Westminster Model systems go even further by enshrining the concept of parliamentary supremacy in which the nation's highest court may issue a ruling, but it can be reversed by a simple act of parliament. (The role of the judiciary is considered further in Chapter 7.)

Could federalism serve as a check on a prime minister? As seen in Chapter 3, federal systems usually designate specifically particular areas of authority for the national and the state or provincial governments. Within those areas designated as solely under national control, states or provinces have few tools to challenge a prime minister. Within the areas of concurrent jurisdiction, states and provinces might be able to curb or limit the authority of a prime minister, although various constitutional supremacy doctrines and the superior resources of the national government may still provide the prime minister with the upper hand. Thus, the prime minister of a federal state might have less comprehensive powers than one in a unitary state, at least on certain domestic issues.

One final possibility to consider is whether some supranational entities can check the actions of a prime minister. Even two decades ago, the answer would have been "no" because national sovereignty generally trumped all other considerations. Today, the answer is a qualified yes, in that once a country has willingly entered into an international treaty or multinational organization, it may well be bound by rulings from outside sources. This is particularly the case with strong organizations such as the European Union and the World Trade Organization that have the power to enforce their rulings. That said, member states within these organizations usually have recourse to a variety of strategies to appeal and delay such rulings and, at the extreme, always have the right to withdraw. In addition, many areas of crucial national concern are exempted from international agreements.

A Hypothetical Case Study:
Parliamentary Checks and Balances

Suppose that a prime minister wished to double his or her country's existing gasoline tax in order to build new highways. Could the prime minister's construction bill be challenged—or halted—and if so how, when, and by whom? Because specifics vary from country to country, the following is a generalized case study.

- The head of state would likely be limited simply to officially approving the bill once it had been passed by the parliament.
- The Cabinet would have the opportunity to discuss and debate the bill in closed session, perhaps offering modifications and counterarguments. But the prime minister would generally still be able to introduce the bill, and after that, all cabinet members would be required to support it or else lose their positions.
- Parliamentary backbenchers of the prime minister's party (or allied parties) in the lower house probably stand nothing to gain and much to lose (such as damaging their own careers) by opposing the bill, so they are unlikely to challenge it.
- The opposition parties in the lower house may loathe the bill, and may say so loudly and publicly. They may even gain an electoral advantage on the issue when the next election is held. But until then, they are powerless to stop the prime minister.
- The upper house of parliament may have the opportunity to delay the bill, to suggest amendments to it, or to hold public hearings criticizing the bill. But if it comes to an outright confrontation between the two houses, the upper house is unlikely to prevail.
- The states or provinces in a federal system may (or may not) have some say over how the funds are allocated in the highways that pass through their territories. But as to the actual passage of the bill, they are unlikely to have much influence because the

action is being taken by the national government on its own authority.

- The court system may be asked to adjudicate various elements of the bill at some later point, but unless and until that happens, it will have little say. And in some countries, parliaments are free to override court decisions if they wish.

- International agreements are likely to be silent regarding internal revenue and infrastructure. In any case, international agreements can be very hard to enforce over the will of an elected national government.

- The electorate, of course, will have the final say in the next election, and public opinion may sway a prime minister. But during the life of a parliament, the voters have no direct control and many prime ministers defy short-term public opinion in hopes of bringing voters around to their position before the next election.

In sum, then, a prime minister may be challenged and constrained by multiple political actors, but a determined prime minister is unlikely to be stopped. Unlike an American president who must contend with the U.S. House, the U.S. Senate, and a federal court system with judicial review, prime ministers are able to act much more unilaterally.

Prime Ministerial Accountability to Parliament

At this stage, it may seem that prime ministers have unfettered power. Unencumbered by the elaborate web of checks and balances that limits U.S. presidents, prime ministers usually get their way. Still, there is one Achilles' heel from which prime ministers suffer that presidents do not, and which may serve as the ultimate brake on their actions. As we have seen, presidents are institutionally sealed off from Congress, which limits their ability to control Congress—but also means that they are not required to be accountable to Congress. Indeed, drawing on their own vast array of constitutional and statutory powers, presidents have wide latitude to operate largely independent of Congress.

This is especially true in the conduct of military operations and the making of foreign policy, in which Congress has a very limited say.

Prime ministers, however, are embedded in parliament and are accountable to that institution, which is never more clearly manifest than when ministers are required to appear on the floor of parliament to be publicly questioned by rank-and-file members. Perhaps the best known example of this is the raucous "Prime Minister's Question Time" during which the British prime minister appears in the House of Commons chamber for half an hour every Wednesday. During this televised spectacle, the prime minister is grilled, mocked, cajoled, and otherwise berated by members of the opposition, and also sometimes even their own party, while being cheered and jeered from the back benches. Armed only with a briefing book, prime ministers must spontaneously speak on a wide variety of issues, sometimes making statements that make news headlines. Question Time is a vivid manifestation of the reality that prime ministers hold their positions *only* because they continue to be supported by a majority of the lower house—and can be deposed by parliament. The same is true of all cabinet ministers, who must also answer questions and can be pressured to resign if enough members of parliament are displeased with their work. (To view this remarkable spectacle, visit <www.cspan.org> and click on Prime Minister's Questions.)

To be sure, no prime minister or other minister has anything like the job security enjoyed by the U.S. president, who is guaranteed a fixed term of four years barring death, disability, resignation, or impeachment. Cabinet ministers can simply be removed by the prime minister. The removal of a prime minister from office is a more complicated affair and, other than by losing an election, can occur in either of two principal ways. The first way would be if enough members of parliament from the prime minister's party (or party coalition) were to decide that the PM is leading them in the wrong direction on policy or has become a liability for the next election. Because the prime minister's sole personal claim to power is the support of a majority in parliament, once that claim is lost, the prime minister can no longer remain in office.

Most prime ministers are acutely aware of their standing within their party, and use their considerable powers to threaten those who would challenge their leadership and to reward their supporters. But it was a challenge from within her own party that toppled even as prominent a figure as the British Prime Minister Margaret Thatcher, who for eleven years concentrated enormous power to herself—so much so that other members of her party long felt that their views were not being heeded. With growing evidence that she was becoming an electoral liability in forthcoming elections, a rare but successful "backbench revolt" was fomented against Thatcher led by a rival whom she had earlier vanquished. Under the imminent threat of replacement as prime minister, the Iron Lady stepped aside in favor of her preferred successor, John Major. Sometimes, a more carefully orchestrated hand-off can also occur between elections, as in 2003 when Canadian Prime Minister Jean Chretien more or less willingly handed over the prime minister's office to his Liberal Party colleague Paul Martin. Similarly, in June 2007, British Prime Minister Tony Blair stepped down in favor of his longtime rival Gordon Brown with hopes of reviving the electoral standing of the Labour Party. (Less dramatically, a prime minister can also be quickly replaced without an election if he or she dies in office, resigns for health or other nonpolitical reasons, or becomes disabled.)

Replacement of the prime minister as party leader, while at times dramatic, is actually the less volatile way to bring about a change in leadership. The other mechanism—called a "vote of no confidence"—topples not just the prime minister but also the entire cabinet of ministers (the government) and usually triggers a new election whose results can be hard to predict. Recall that executive power in a parliamentary system is drawn solely from the support, or confidence, of a majority in the lower house of parliament. Should the government lose a vote in parliament, this can either be taken as evidence that the government has lost majority support, or it can trigger a special vote in parliament to determine whether that is indeed the case. If the parliamentary vote reveals the loss of majority, the government is said to have "fallen" or "collapsed," which is not nearly as dire an event as it sounds to American ears. An election will then be held to get a new mandate from the people. Paul Martin's prime ministership in Canada, for example, proved quite short-lived, and his government was toppled by a vote of no confidence in late 2004.

Votes of no confidence are unusual when one party holds a majority and, thus, has the less radical option of simply replacing the prime minister rather than run the risk of calling a new election which the party might lose. Votes of no confidence are much more likely in coalition governments, where the defection of any one party can lead to a loss of a parliamentary majority. The more parties that are in a coalition, the greater this danger because as a government makes real-world decisions, it can become harder and harder to please all groups. Further, the smaller the party, the narrower its electoral base and the more likely it is to have a few deeply entrenched interests that are non-negotiable to it. Thus, if a party coalition that relies on a small rural-based party must also bring in a city-based party to survive, the two may have irreconcilable goals. If the government must decide between preserving countryside or expanding urban zones, for instance, the small party on the losing side may no longer see any advantage to remaining in the coalition and trigger a vote of no confidence.

The ability of a parliament to topple a prime minister, and his or her government, at any time can go a long way toward reining in prime ministers and promoting democratic participation. In the United States, Congress does have the power to impeach and remove the president from office, but this cannot constitutionally be done purely out of political disagreement; it is usually based on evidence of "high crimes and misdemeanors." The 1998–1999 impeachment and trial of Bill Clinton represented a troubling break with the tradition of reserving the congressional removal power for serious abuse of power, both because Clinton's offenses were comparatively minor and because they had no relationship to his role as president. But even in this highly partisan proceeding, the Senate did not come close to reaching the two-third majority required to remove Clinton. The impeachment and conviction powers of the Congress involve an arduous process that is a far cry from a parliamentary vote of no confidence.

The ability to topple governments at any time certainly can also have some negative consequences in terms of stability. Perhaps the most notorious example of this is Italy, where a highly fragmented party system has meant that coalition governments of six, eight, or more parties are the norm. In the sixty-year period between the formation of a democratic government at the end of World War II and 2006, Italy had more than sixty governments, most lasting less than a year. Indeed, it was not until the period 2001–2006 that any government survived for its entire five-year term (only to be narrowly defeated when elections were called). This extreme pattern of instability fostered a sense of chaos in the politics of the nation and contributed mightily to the persistent inability of the Italian state to effectively address such problems as extreme regional inequalities, entrenched corruption, the mafia and other types of organized crime, and terrorism by both right-wing and left-wing political factions.

Another element offering greater stability in the United States is fixed-term elections. Since the first unanimous election of George Washington, a president has been elected exactly every four years, as have members of Congress every two years. Once a U.S. presidential election is held, it is impossible for there to be another until another four years have passed. Most likely, the person elected president will serve out the term, but if not it will almost surely be a senior politician from the same political party, namely the vice president. The composition of Congress is nearly as stable, even if a few individual members might change between regularly scheduled elections. Such executive and legislative stability is in stark contrast to that found in parliamentary systems, especially those with multiparty coalition governments. Patterns of change are, thus, far more predictable under the United States system, enabling longer-range planning and fostering a sense that elected officials have a legitimate right to govern for the duration of their terms.

Despite their contribution to stability, however, fixed terms of office also add an element of rigidity to the political system, making it all but impossible to replace a president who proves to be ineffectual or a Congress which is paralyzed or deadlocked, before the next regularly scheduled election. President Jimmy Carter was widely considered to be ineffective for at least the last two years of his term, yet there was no way to replace him with a leader better suited to the challenges the country was facing. If he had been a prime minister, Bill Clinton would probably not have survived in office after his sex scandal with Monica Lewinsky, sparing the country more than a year of distractions. And the strongly pro-Democratic vote in the Congressional elections of 2006 amounted to a vote of no confidence in

President George W. Bush and his policies, yet Bush remained in office as commander-in-chief.

In all, the fusion of powers in a parliamentary system offers some significant strengths when compared with the U.S. system. Almost by definition, the sort of divided government that is often found in the United States—such as a Democratic president and a Republican-controlled Congress—cannot occur in a parliamentary system (especially when the upper house is clearly subordinate to the lower house). Even when the United States experiences unified government—when the White House and both Houses of Congress are under the control of the same party—they are still institutionally separated, and there is no guarantee of cooperation. This was seen vividly in the failure of the ambitious Clinton health care program in 1993, for instance, when both Congress and the presidency were controlled by Democrats. More recently, conflict between the branches despite party affiliations was seen in 2005 and 2006 with the demise of President George W. Bush's plans to overhaul Social Security and to reform immigration policy at a time when his Republican Party controlled both the Senate and the House of Representatives.

Of course, it was part of the original design of the U.S. Constitution for government to be inefficient in order for it not to become tyrannical. Such inefficiency, however, can have deleterious real-world outcomes in the realm of public policy. Health care provides one of the most vivid examples of the failure of the separation-of-powers system in the United States. More than forty million Americans are uninsured and a crisis looms in which tens of millions of baby boomers are likely to need extensive care in their old age. Yet the two Houses of Congress and the president have remained incapable of reforming a cumbersome and inefficient health care system that costs far more per capita than that of any other country in the world.

In a parliamentary system, coordination between the legislative and executive powers is automatic because they are both wielded simultaneously by the same people from the same party (or coalition of parties)—the prime minister and the cabinet. This means that in parliamentary systems, there is much less likely to be inaction—often called "gridlock" because of conflict between different parties and/or different branches of government. Reform of the health care system, or almost anything else, could be accomplished practically overnight. This is not always necessarily an advantage: after several elections, Labour and Conservative governments in Britain successively nationalized and privatized the British steel industry, creating an instability that destroyed its ability to compete internationally. Still, governments of both parties were simply keeping their campaign promises, which were well known to voters before the election.

In fact, one political consequence of the parliamentary system is that voters can much more easily hold political parties accountable for their accomplishments at the next election, a concept called responsible government. In the U.S. system, the president can blame Congress, the House of Representatives can point to the Senate, the state and local governments can excoriate the national government, and all can claim judicial interference, making it hard for voters to know where to place credit or blame. Because of the concentration of power in parliamentary systems (especially in unitary states), the success or failure of any given government is much more readily discerned by the voters. Parliamentary governments have all the tools they need to enact their campaign promises, and the voters are unlikely to be very forgiving if they fail to do so.

Conclusion

Although distinctive executive, legislative, and judicial roles can be found in most of the countries of the world, they are not always—or usually—institutionally separated. The separation of powers system has, on the whole, functioned effectively in the United States, but it has proven much more problematic in other countries. The system of separation of powers has significant implications for the workings of each of the three branches, which are the focus of Part II of this book.

Further Reading

- *Comparative Constitutional Engineering: An Inquiry into Structures, Incentives and Outcomes.* Giovanni Sartori. New York University Press, New York: 1997.

- *Democracies: Patterns of Majoritarian and Consensus Government in Twenty-One Countries.* Arend Lijphardt. Yale University Press, New Haven, CT: 1984.
- *Checks and Balances? How a Parliamentary System Could Change American Politics.* Paul Christopher Manuel and Anne Marie Cammisa. Westview Press, Boulder, CO: 1999.

Web-Based Exploration Exercise

Visit the Web site of any country with a parliamentary system of government. Identify and explain two similarities and two differences between the roles of these parliamentary institutions and their counterparts in the United States. A comprehensive portal to the governmental Web sites of countries around the world can be found at <www.gksoft.com/govt/en/world.html>

Question for Debate and Discussion

While it is possible to generalize about the parliamentary system of government, its actual operation varies significantly from country to country. Some differences are institutional, such as whether the prime minister is largely shielded from votes of no confidence (as in Germany) or has a limited ability to control the cabinet (as in Italy). Other differences are political, such as when minority governments are permitted by the parliamentary opposition to rule (as is fairly common in Scandinavia), or when the extreme fragmentation of the party system makes it difficult to form stable coalitions (as in Israel). Examine the particulars of a parliamentary system with an unusual feature and determine how and why that feature has emerged, then make a direct comparison between that country and the U.S. system.

II

THE INSTITUTIONS
OF GOVERNMENT

5

THE EXECUTIVE BRANCH

The Presidency and the Bureaucracy

The one, indispensable, common element across all forms of government is the existence of executive power—the ability to act backed by the threat or use of force. In the evolution of governing structures of all types, three of the crucial factors have always been the power to muster force of arms, to collect taxes, and to enforce the will of the rulers among the people. In the modern world, another characteristic of all sovereign states is their ability to enter into and conduct relations with other states. And as society has grown more complex, most states have developed executive-branch bureaucracies for regulating and supervising various aspects of the society and economy and for providing programs and services. In some countries, executive power may also extend to direct control of, or at least some, role in the legislative task of writing laws and allocating funds, and the judicial role of interpreting the law.

The same core areas of authority and responsibility can be found in the executives of all functioning states, including the United States. Indeed, it is common to speak of the American president as playing a number of distinct roles encompassing the full range of executive power based on Article II of the U.S. Constitution. In the commander-in-chief role, the president has power to deploy and direct the military. As the chief diplomat, the president has the authority to appoint and receive ambassadors and generally to conduct relations with other countries. In the head-of-government role, the president has the ability to appoint and direct the federal bureaucracy. And as head of state, the president serves as the symbol of the unity of the country and continuity of national history.

Case Study: Variations in Executive Power in Southeast Asia

Executive power may be universal, but the institutional configurations of executive power are many and varied. This variety can be readily seen by examining five neighboring countries of southeast Asia, each with entirely distinctive executive arrangements: Brunei, Malaysia, Indonesia, Myanmar, and Vietnam.

The tiny, oil-rich Sultanate of Brunei represents the most traditional of all forms of executive power: autocratic control by a hereditary monarch. There are no checks or limits of any kind on the extremely wealthy sultan, who is head of state, head of government, commander-in-chief, religious leader, prime minister, minister of defense, and minister of finance. The sultan receives nonbinding advice from various consultative bodies, all of whose members he appoints, and then rules by royal decree.

Malaysia has a robust parliamentary system, with a clear-cut division between the head of government and head of state roles. A former British colony with a highly diverse population, Malaysia has adopted a system quite similar to the Westminster parliamentary model, with effective executive power exerted by a prime minister who is the leader of the majority in the lower house of a bicameral legislature. The prime minister serves as head of government and appoints and directs a cabinet to oversee the military, foreign affairs, and other various government ministries. The prime minister is not the head of state, however; that role is played by a king whose responsibilities are chiefly ceremonial and religious.

In nearby Indonesia, a country consisting of an archipelago of thousands of islands and home to the fourth largest population in the world, the system is much more akin to that found in the United States, especially since major constitutional reforms in 2004. Today, the country has a strict separation-of-powers system, with a president who is directly elected by the people and who appoints and directs the work of a cabinet of ministers. The Indonesian president directly carries out all four of the principal executive roles: head of state, commander-in-chief, chief diplomat, and head of government. Much as in the United States, the president must contend with an elected, bicameral legislature, one house of which is elected based on population and the other based on regional representation, with joint lawmaking powers. Having become a multiparty democracy only after the forced 1998 resignation of longtime military-backed dictator Mohammed Suharto, the future of executive power in Indonesia remains uncertain.

One possible, and troubling, trajectory for Indonesia is the situation found in Myanmar (formerly Burma) where a group of military officers rules the country by force, with no constitution, no legislature, no independent judiciary, and no other checks and balances on their decrees. Through a State Peace and Development Council, the military officers appoint one among their number to serve as prime minister and also appoint a cabinet, judges, and regional governments, all subject to the officers' will. The elected People's Assembly has been prevented from meeting since 1990 and the nation's democratically elected leader, Nobel Peace Prize-winner Aung San Suu Kyi, has been under kept under house arrest. Utterly unresponsive to their own people, as well as to the international community, Myanmar's military leaders have turned their country into an international pariah—and an unusually blunt throwback to the concept of might-makes-right.

Might also makes right in neighboring Vietnam, although the exercise of executive power is much more elaborately justified by the Communist Party, which has concentrated all authority to itself since 1975. Constitutionally, executive authority is wielded by a president who serves as head of state and a prime minister who is head of government. But in practice, Vietnam continues to exercise the system prevalent in the former Soviet Union even some fifteen years after the demise of that country: real power resides with officials of the Communist Party. In this regard, then, the president, prime minister, and other ministers are not independent executive actors but are more akin to government bureaucrats who implement and administer programs and policies that are set by the Party.

Nondemocratic Executives

In the contemporary world, the case of Brunei is extreme in the absolute powers invested in the sultan, but several other, primarily also
Muslim, countries invest their kings with final authority. To one
degree or another, these include Morocco, Saudi Arabia, Jordan, the
United Arab Emirates, Oman, Qatar, and Kuwait. Some of these
states may have written constitutions, elected legislatures, and federal
structures, and their day-to-day governance may be carried out by an
appointed prime minister and a professional government, but these are
all clearly subject to the authority of the throne. Even absent checks
and balances, however, monarchs rarely have the ability to act entirely
unilaterally. The king of Saudi Arabia, for instance, can make compelling religious and historical claims to power but must still consider
the demands of the 7,000 or so royal princes who are descendants of
the nation's founder. And despite tight control over the media and the
near-total absence of political participation by the people, Saudi leaders must also keep a close eye on the needs and wishes of their own
people—if only to prevent the kind of revolution that toppled the once
equally powerful shah in neighboring Iran.

In some other countries, executive power is monopolized by a single political faction, often one that emerged victorious from an era of
revolution or civil war. After World War II, these factions were often
Communist Parties, although most of these have since fallen from
power. However, the Communist Party still predominates in Vietnam as well as in Laos, China, and North Korea in Asia, plus Cuba
in the Caribbean; in such countries, one party monopolizes all power
both in theory and in practice. Many other non-Communist countries, particularly in Africa and the Middle East, allow the appearance of multiparty elections but in practice maintain tight rule by a
single faction—and often by a single dictator. Election results may be
tampered with, or the political system may be structured so that other
forces are effectively prevented access to media, funding, or other factors needed to really contest elections. The general population is often
kept acquiescent through a combination of heavy-handed media cen-
sorship, threats to their jobs and livelihoods, and police forces able to
act with impunity.

The circumstances surrounding rule by a single party vary quite widely. Some dictators have so totally consolidated their personal power that they can act largely as they wish, at least within their own borders; Kim Jong Il of North Korea, Fidel Castro of Cuba, and Muammar Khadafi of Libya fall into that category. In other cases, longtime near-dictatorial rulers such as Robert Mugabe of Zimbabwe and Hosni Mubarak of Egypt must carefully balance—and at times brutally suppress—countervailing forces within their own countries. In countries with more collective types of leadership, such as the Community Party elite of China or the Islamic mullahs in Iran, leaders must vie with and accommodate other members of their own ruling faction even while marginalizing other contenders for power.

The case of rule by raw military force, as in Myanmar, is relatively rare as of 2007. Only a handful of countries, such as Pakistan and Sudan, now have generals clearly atop their political hierarchies. In many countries, however, the armed forces are capable of independent action and may intervene directly in the political system from time to time, at times even deposing elected officials and installing generals or puppet civilians into executive office. Typically, the army tries to argue some patriotic justification for their intervention, such as suppressing separatists, or subversives, or counterrevolutionaries, or more recently, terrorists. Military regimes lack the legitimacy of traditional monarchies or even single-party states, however, and often resort to brute-force tactics of intimidation, torture, and murder. Militaries also rarely have the skills or inclination needed to manage an entire country, and economic and social problems tend to proliferate under their leadership, often leading to an eventual return to civilian government—a cyclical pattern that has been especially prevalent in Central and South America. The generals that brutally, and incompetently, ruled Argentina on and off for nearly three decades finally fell in 1982 when they spectacularly failed even at a military objective, seizing control of the Falkland Islands (Las Malvinas) from the British.

This discussion of executive power in nondemocratic countries is relatively brief because such systems are unable to shed much light on the politics of the United States. First off, the American president is emphatically not a monarch. Having just fought a war of independence, the founders rejected any thought of installing a hereditary king or even of a highly powerful executive with lifetime tenure of office. Crucial early precedents set by George Washington, such as declining to be called "Your Majesty" and voluntarily stepping down from office after two terms, further underscored that the president is a citizen, not a monarch. With the possible exception of the president's unilateral power to grant pardons—a holdover from monarchical practices—all presidential powers are subject to multiple checks and balances. A strong tradition of noninterference in politics by the U.S. military and its very limited role on U.S. soil have prevented it from becoming either the servant, or the master, of American presidents.

The U.S. presidency has also never been a platform for anything close to single-party rule. Electoral cycles and patterns of voter allegiance have from time to time consolidated the rule of one party or another. Notably, the presidency was held by the Democratic Party for all but eight years from 1933 to 1969 and by the Republican Party for all but sixteen years from 1897 to 1933 and all but twelve years from 1969 to at least 2009. Still, during these periods opposition party candidates won seven out of twenty-seven presidential elections, and also had influence in Congress and at the state level. The U.S. presidency has also never become a platform for personal rule by the president. Richard Nixon egregiously abused his office, covering up break-ins of the offices of the Democratic Party and ordering the IRS to audit his political enemies, and also promulgated an "Imperial Presidency" by disregarding the will of Congress and acting secretly in the prosecution of the Vietnam War. Ultimately, Nixon was, of course, forced to resign the presidency under the immediate threat of impeachment and removal from office, although only after many months of political paralysis and nearly a constitutional crisis.

Democratic Dual Executives

Although the U.S. presidency bears little resemblance to the executive power in most nondemocratic countries, its institutional contours are also quite different from those found in most other democratic countries. Indeed, of the twenty-two countries that have been continuously democratic since 1950, only Costa Rica also concentrates all executive power in a single individual who is entirely separated from the legislature. The others, including nearly all of the countries of Europe, all have a dual executive with one person filling the ceremonial role of head of state and another acting as head of government, deriving authority as prime ministers from control of a majority in parliament. (The executive role of prime ministers is discussed in some detail in Chapter 4 and, therefore, is excluded from this chapter.)

In systems with dual executives, the head of state role historically originated with powerful kingships, and today a number of these countries retain hereditary constitutional monarchs who play a ceremonial and symbolic role while all real power resides with prime ministers and cabinets drawn from parliament. These constitutional monarchs carry out such formal public functions that offer continuity and legitimacy to the government. Thus, for instance, most constitutional monarchs officially open sessions of parliament and some proclaim the government's agenda from the throne, amid great grandeur and rich tradition. They may also formally appoint the prime minister and other ministers, provide their assent to legislation and treaties, act as the ceremonial commander-in-chief of the armed forces, and officially receive foreign ambassadors assigned to their countries, all without exerting actual influence over the substance of the work of government. Constitutional monarchs sometimes in theory retain wide-ranging reserve powers, such as to reject legislation or issue orders to the military, but they know that if they were to ever actually try to exercise them, it would most likely lead to the abolition of the monarchy.

Kings and queens may have a special claim to represent historical continuity and the enduring values of the state, but what of those parliamentary democracies that do not have their own monarch? With only rare exceptions, those countries have chosen *not* to make their prime minister into the head of state, but rather to create new structures. In a number of countries of the former British Empire, such as Canada, Australia, and New Zealand, a governor-general is appointed by the prime minister from the local population to fill in for the queen as ceremonial head of state, with essentially the same responsibilities and limitations.

A more common solution is to create as figurehead a president to serve as head of state, in somewhat pale imitations of ceremonial monarchs. Although the specifics vary widely, ceremonial presidents generally wield little or no independent authority. Most, such as the presidents of Germany and Israel, are elected by the parliament; a few, such as in Austria and Ireland, are directly elected by the people, although this popular mandate does not particularly enhance their constitutional powers. Generally, ceremonial presidents are respected and accomplished individuals in the society—central bankers, prominent journalists, retired politicians, famous artists—who are intended to be above politics.

In times of crisis, heads of state may also play an important stabilizing role, particularly when democratic practices are not well established or are under threat. In 1981, King Juan Carlos of Spain used his role as commander-in-chief of the military to make a television broadcast ordering an end to an attempted military coup during which senior officers had seized control of the parliament. Heads of state, particularly monarchs, can also offer political legitimacy and continuity to governments that are disrupted by foreign invasion or civil war. Several European kings did this during World War II, and more recently the exiled King Mohammed Zahir Shah played this role in Afghanistan when a post-Taliban government was established there in 2002, albeit without his reclaiming the throne.

Even in less extreme circumstances, heads of state can also play an important role as neutral political arbitrators. Indeed, the one key nonceremonial responsibility of the head of state is to ensure that there is always a head of government. This is usually not a concern because most parliamentary elections produce a clear winning party or coalition of parties. Then, the head of state simply can—indeed must—invite the head of the winning party or coalition to form a government. If no clear legislative majority emerges after an election, the head of state may assist in negotiations to help form a new governing coalition. Likewise, after a vote of no confidence, a head of state may delay the dissolution of parliament in hopes that a new majority can be found without the need for a new election. In the case of real deadlock, some heads of state may play a hands-on role as a political broker and might even exercise personal discretion in choosing whom to invite to form a government. This has been the case particularly in parliaments composed of many fractious parties, such as Italy and Israel. Still, the choice of prime minister is always subject to a confirmatory vote by parliament. And even if there is an absolute impasse and negotiations fail, the head of state would still never take direct power. The previous prime minister and cabinet, or a temporary replacement, would generally continue to exercise executive authority in a caretaker capacity with the head of state calling new elections with hopes that a revote would decisively change the balance in parliament.

It should be noted that a number of countries with parliaments have chosen both to directly elect their presidents *and* to invest them with a significant degree of real power, an arrangement often called a semipresidential system. Since 1958, the president of France has been directly elected by the people as head of state, commander-in-chief, and chief diplomat. The president also directly appoints the prime minister, who must be confirmed by parliament. When there is a parliamentary majority of the same party as the president, final executive authority is, in practice, wielded by the president; at other times it becomes necessary for the president to name a prime minister from the majority party and for the two to share power under an arrangement called "cohabitation."

Such a situation is awkward, although France has generally handled it well. More problematic has been the case of the Palestinian Authority in 2007, in which a moderate president from one party and a radical prime minister from another both claimed executive authority, leading to civil strife. By contrast, in Russia the post-Soviet semipresidential system has, under Vladimir Putin, become a vehicle for overwhelming concentration of power in the presidency, with the prime minister and parliament almost wholly subordinate. For exactly these reasons, few established democracies employ a semipresidential system, with some countries such as Greece, Finland, and Portugal moving away from that model toward a more standard parliamentary system.

The American Presidency in Comparative Perspective

As seen in the examples from Southeast Asia, executive power can take many configurations. The U.S. presidency is but one of those configurations, and it combines a number of different attributes seen in the case studies, along with some specific features of its own. United States presidents enjoy enormous democratic legitimacy because they are elected directly by the people (albeit via the rather problematic Electoral College) and are also the only elected officials (along with their hand-picked vice presidents) who represent the entire country. Further, presidents have a fixed term of office independent of any actions of other political actors. This makes U.S. presidents quite unlike prime ministers, who are not directly elected by the people, who represent just one of many districts, and who hold their office only as long as they retain the support of a parliamentary majority.

Of course, the U.S. presidency (and those presidencies that draw on the U.S. model, especially in Latin America) is also unusual in that it concentrates essentially *all* executive roles and authority in a single individual. But does it matter that the U.S. president is expected to simultaneously play a symbolic role as head of state while also being immersed in day-to-day politics as head of government? From a purely pragmatic perspective, the answer is probably no. Because heads of state in other countries generally play little or no role in practical politics, they can largely be overlooked when seeking to understand the workings of government. But the investiture of head of state responsibilities in the U.S. presidency serves in other, more subtle, ways to alter the essential nature of the office. Even as they are criticized in the press and parodied in popular culture, U.S. presidents also enjoy a tremendous degree of deference and respect, viewed at once as ordinary politicians and yet also as figures who are in some contexts above everyday politics. The so-called bully pulpit of the president—the ability to garner attention and shape public opinion—is greater than that of most prime ministers, who are always immersed in workaday politics. Yet it can also mean that the president is held to higher personal and professional standards. In many ways, the 1999 impeachment of Bill Clinton was framed much more about his violation of the dignity of his office than any abuse of presidential power or other serious offense.

The head of state role of the U.S. presidency is most clearly manifested in the annual State of the Union address, when the president addresses the nation from the dais of the House of Representatives. Certainly this triumphal occasion, attended by the Congress, Cabinet, Supreme Court, top military officers, and the foreign diplomatic corps, is a far cry from the often merciless grilling on the floor of parliament to which prime ministers are subjected every week. In fact, it more closely resembles the "throne speech" that is read by constitutional monarchs (although written by the government of the day) at the annual opening of parliament. The ceremonial role of the presidency also rises to the fore in times of crisis, such the September 11 terrorist attacks, after which George W. Bush spoke at a prayer service in the National Cathedral. No other social or political figure in the country has anywhere near comparable standing to address and lead the nation in troubled times, when public opinion tends to rally round the flag by providing soaring approval ratings to presidents whatever their actual actions.

The fusion of head of state and head of government roles clearly strengthens the position of the U.S. presidency (and other presidencies based on the American model), enabling presidents to mobilize public opinion and pressure and giving them leverage over Congress and other political actors. This fusion also has a number of problematic effects as well. For instance, the symbolic role of the president as leader of the nation clearly influences who can be elected to the office. A disengaged but visionary leader such as Ronald Reagan would rarely if ever be found in a prime ministerial office, but was well suited to the American head of state role. Countries with parliamentary systems seem more ready to accept leaders who are politically adept and technically skilled but who may be less than charismatic or who do not connect with the public on an emotional level. The need to be widely perceived and accepted as a potential leader of the nation also affects which U.S. presidential candidacies are even deemed viable—and may help to explain why American presidents have always been men of European extraction and, with one exception, Protestant religion.

Even more troubling is that making the president the head of state can make it difficult to separate the person from the office—and the office from the state itself. In Britain, this distinction is nicely captured by the convention of calling the members of the party that is out of power "Her Majesty's Loyal Opposition," stressing that they oppose the government of the day but not the state. In the United States, by contrast, Richard Nixon famously (and inaccurately) argued that anything the president does is by definition legal. In the aftermath of September 11, some White House staff members went so far as to suggest that questioning the president in times of crisis was intrinsically unpatriotic, even bordering on the treasonous. In countries with a dual executive, however, it is much easier to distinguish between the particular politician currently serving as head of government and the more enduring values of the state itself. And, of course, the fact that prime ministers are ultimately responsible to—and can be replaced by—parliaments also keeps in check their ability to aggrandize their own power and status.

Other Presidential Systems

The United States has mostly managed to navigate the dangers of fusing the head of state and head of government roles, but most other countries with presidential systems have not been so fortunate. The separation-of-powers system, with a directly elected president and a separate bicameral Congress, is by far the predominant system adopted throughout Latin America. This is in part because of the historical influence of the United States as a neighboring country, but also because the other countries of the western hemisphere found themselves in a similar historical situation as the United States. After achieving independence from Spain or Portugal, the countries of Latin America generally saw no more compelling reason to separate the two roles than did the United States. And far more so than in the United States, many Latin countries had strong traditions of rule by *caudillos* or powerful individual leaders.

In general, the presidential system has not proven an effective means for Latin American countries to deal with the often severe poverty, gross inequalities, endemic corruption, and other challenges they face. When legislatures, courts, interest groups, and the general public are politically active, Latin American presidents have often found themselves too weak institutionally. In some cases, this has led to political paralysis, and a loss of legitimacy for the government, leading to further social and political problems and, often, interventions and coups by military generals. In other cases, Latin American presidents have made use of their control of the military and police to declare states of emergency, suspend constitutional rights, dissolve parliaments, and rule by executive decree. This pattern is typified by the Latin American president who is perhaps best known around the world, the populist Juan Peron, who ruled Argentina for ten tumultuous years after World War II. Working within a constitutional framework explicitly modeled on that of the United States, Peron and his political party nonetheless completely dominated all sectors of Argentine society, corralling public opinion, marginalizing congress, manipulating the courts, and either co-opting or suppressing his political opponents. His strongman rule laid the groundwork for the three decades of direct power by the military over Argentine government, including periods of brutal dictatorship.

The vacillation between excessively weak democratic presidents and excessively strong anti-democratic presidents has contributed greatly to internal conflict, governmental corruption, and political repression throughout Latin America. Presidential systems have similarly failed in other parts of the world. An example would be those African countries which rejected parliamentary systems after their decolonization in the 1950s and 1960s in favor of strong presidencies that have served as vehicles for personal dictatorships, one-party states, and military rule. In the 1970s and 80s, dictators from Idi Amin of Uganda, to Jean-Bedel Bokassa of the Central African Republic, to Haile Mariam Mengistu of Ethiopia terrorized their populations with actions ranging from localized massacres to outright genocides. More recently, the shocking memory of these brutalities has helped to curb autocratic governments and promote multiparty democracy across Africa, although the future of democracy on the continent remains uncertain.

There may be times, particularly in regimes undergoing a transitional phase, when a strong presidency offers benefits. In post-Taliban Afghanistan, the new constitution created a powerful, independently elected president because power in the country was at that time fragmented among multiple competing warlords controlling various regions. One hope was that a strong president could serve as a symbolic rallying point and unifying symbol, which President Hamid Karzai appears to have achieved to some degree. But, as of this writing, he has not been able to assert effective military or political control outside the capital city, leading some to dub him the Mayor of Kabul.

The U.S. Vice President, Cabinet, and Bureaucracy

Although all executive power in the United States is vested constitutionally in one person, the U.S. president is not the only actor in the executive branch. Of these other actors, the U.S. vice president is one of the most anomalous of all the structures created by the Constitution. For most of American history, the sole tasks of the vice president were from time to time to ceremonially preside over the Senate and break the occasional tie vote—and to wait for the president to die. In recent decades, vice presidents have evolved into senior advisors to the president, assisting with policy formulation, political salesmanship, and some ceremonial duties. Vice Presidents Walter Mondale, George H.W. Bush, Al Gore, and especially, Dick Cheney have exercised influence well beyond what their nonexistent constitutional authority would suggest possible.

In general, however, vice presidents are a nonessential feature of presidential systems and, indeed, can pose a danger in less established democracies if they conspire to seize the presidency. In fact, Mexico abolished the office in the nineteenth century after a number of vice presidents supported coups that enabled them to ascend to the top job. (In one forty-year period, Mexico had more than fifty short-lived presidencies.) One advantage of a vice-presidential office is that it enables the party in power to stay in power should a president die, resign, be removed from office, or be temporarily disabled, all without the need for a special election. Unfortunately, vice presidents are often chosen not for their governing skills, but for their appeal in elections or, worse, because they are perceived as politically weak and thus not as a potential threat to the president. Countries without vice presidents are generally able to find other satisfactory ways to fill a presidential vacancy, such as temporary replacement followed by a quick special election, while suffering no great loss to their governing structures.

Beyond the vice president and perhaps some high-ranking members of the White House Staff, the most high profile figures in the executive branch are the members of the president's Cabinet—the heads of fifteen of the largest departments in the federal government. Some of these are relatively small departments dealing with functional areas of the economy, such as commerce, transportation, and energy.

However, some of the cabinet positions can be extremely influential, particularly those that closely relate to core functions of government, including the Secretaries of State, Defense, and Treasury, as well as the Attorney General, who leads the Department of Justice. Many cabinet secretaries have had impressive careers of their own, as governors, senators, generals, business leaders, or other prominent roles.

As significant as these cabinet figures may be, however, their relationship to the president is entirely unambiguous; they are chosen by the president to advance the president's agenda and can be directed, reassigned, and dismissed, serving only "at the president's pleasure," as the phrase goes. *All* executive authority exercised by members of the Cabinet, the heads of non-Cabinet executive agencies, and indeed by members of the federal bureaucracy (except for a few regulatory commissions) technically is carried out on behalf of the president. While they may rely on the guidance and expertise of members of the Cabinet and other top-level officials, presidents are completely free to disregard such counsel if they wish.

This idea of a cabinet is quite different from the way that term is used in the parliamentary tradition, in which members of a cabinet—that is to say, the ministers who direct major government bureaucracies—generally must also be sitting members of the majority in parliament. Far more than in the United States, parliamentary cabinet ministers are chosen because of their political standing and support rather than their substantive expertise. Most ministers in parliamentary systems are long-seated members of the party who are well-established politicians in their own right, often formally or informally heading factions within parliament. This was long the case in Japan, where the Liberal Democratic Party has ruled for all but ten months of the last half century. Despite this seeming monopoly control, the existence of multiple intraparty factions has meant that power in Japan is in fact dispersed across many different ministries with prime ministers merely being first among equals. A similar situation pertains in countries such as Israel and Italy where the cooperation of multiple small parties is usually needed to assemble a majority coalition. In these cases, prime ministers must fill their cabinets with leaders of many parties and engage in ongoing negotiations to keep small parties from withdrawing from the coalition and triggering a vote of no confidence.

The parliamentary system also affects how cabinet ministers relate to the bureaucrats in their ministries. In the United States, the entire top tier of government is essentially decapitated after each presidential election, often making for chaotic transitions between presidential administrations. All of the officials at the several highest levels of the U.S. federal bureaucracy are political appointees, and it is standing practice that they will resign their offices upon the completion of the term of the president who appointed them. It is only several layers down from the top of each department or program in the United States that one finds long-term civil servants who are insulated from dismissal for political reasons.

Parliamentary systems, in contrast, are likely to have ministries with two heads: the elected minister and a civil servant (sometimes called a "director-general") who is the permanent chief of the bureaucracy. The job of the elected minister, perhaps with a few junior ministers also drawn from parliament, is to express the political will of the government and to oversee the general direction of a particular ministry. The director-general, by contrast, is a technical specialist who will have served many different governments over decades, providing a note of continuity amid parliamentary majorities that come and go, sometimes quite abruptly. In theory, the director-general and his or her bureaucratic subordinates are nonpartisan, politically neutral servants of the state who simply respond to the elected government of the day. In most cases, they are chosen through a competitive system of exams and promoted for their technical expertise rather than their political ties. Of course, in practice, bureaucracies do have their own political preferences and, even more so, their own established way of doing things. The minister of the day may at worst be viewed as a passing nuisance to be managed and outlasted rather than obeyed. In the United States, placement of political appointees in so many top-tier jobs in the bureaucracy diminishes its autonomy from political control. Yet another level of supervision is created by the oversight of the federal bureaucracy by standing committees of Congress, which can alter programs' funding, organization, or authority.

Another difference between the U.S. bureaucracy and that of many other countries is its size. The United States has a much smaller national bureaucracy than in other wealthy countries, particularly outside the realm of defense (which is proportionately much larger in the United States than in most other democracies). Indeed, the United States has long had an ideology of small government, preferring to leave many areas to the private sector (and to adjudication in the courts) rather than to create new government programs to directly administer them. The strongly federal nature of the United States may help to mask the extent of bureaucracy, however, because state, county, and local governments in the United States also administer extensive government programs. State and local governments tend to have the same basic structure as the federal government, with a single, directly elected governor or mayor naming all the top bureaucrats as political appointees to lead a permanent civil service.

The comparatively modest size of government bureaucracy in the United States, and its scattering across fifty states, more than 3,000 counties, and nearly 20,000 municipalities, means that a powerful, unified national civil service has never emerged in the United States. By comparison, in some unitary states with large bureaucracies, such as France and Japan, the civil service plays a powerful quasi-autonomous role in the political system, positions are highly coveted, and many young people aspire to government jobs. Indeed, drawn from top educational institutions and recruited through dense personal networks, civil servants in some countries constitute an elite corps that is highly influential in many sectors of society. In the United States, being a civil servant is not particularly prestigious, and many of the most ambitious people in the society gravitate instead toward powerful elected positions or influential slots in the private sector.

Conclusion

The office of president of the United States has been occupied in unbroken succession for nearly 220 years, making it history's oldest democratic executive. Because of the military, diplomatic, and economic power of the United States, the American president is perhaps the most prominent political office in the world. Yet it is also an atypical one in many respects: most established democracies do not have U.S.-style presidencies, and most countries that have adopted the system have found it an all-too-convenient platform for dictatorship. To be successful, an office this powerful must be checked and balanced by other powerful political actors. Fortunately, the United States also has developed exactly such active and robust institutions in its Congress and Supreme Court, the subjects of the next two chapters.

Further Reading

- *Chief Executives: National Political Leadership in the United Sates, Mexico Great Britain, Germany, and Japan.* Taketsugu Tsurutani and Jack B. Gabbert, Eds. Washington State University Press, Pullman, WA: 1992.
- *Political Leadership in Liberal Democracies.* Robert Elgie. St. Martin's Press, New York: 1995.
- *Comparative Bureaucratic Systems.* Krishna K. Tummala, Ed. Lexington Books, New York: 2003.

Web-Based Exploration Exercise

Visit the Web site of the White House (<www.whitehouse.gov>) and find examples of recent activities of the president in the four major roles of the office: head of state, chief diplomat, commander-in-chief of the armed forces, and head of the federal bureaucracy. Explain how each of these activities might, or might not, have been carried out differently if the United States had a parliamentary system.

Question for Debate and Discussion

The separation-of-powers system has been criticized for creating presidencies that are either too weak or too powerful. Hemmed in by pressure from the legislative and judicial branches, some presidents are unable to effectively lead. Institutionally insulated from other political actors, some presidents abuse their power and disregard, or dominate, other political actors. Is the U.S. presidency too weak or too strong? Should the U.S. presidency be changed to strengthen or weaken the office?

6

THE LEGISLATIVE BRANCH

The Two Houses of Congress

In the last chapter, we saw that executive power is always relevant in the study of governments: all functioning states have a significant role for the executive in carrying out the work of government. By contrast, the role of legislatures varies widely. At one extreme are powerless assemblies convened purely to provide a show of support for the work of an authoritarian executive. In between are legislatures whose work is mostly consultative or technical, providing input and suggestions but deferring most actual decision making to the executive, whether a prime minister chosen from their own ranks or a separately elected president. Finally, there are legislatures that are fully autonomous and who exercise considerable power within their sphere of influence. The U.S. Congress, the most powerful national legislature in the world, is the paradigmatic example of the last category of legislatures.

The U.S. Congress has sweeping powers to pass laws on issues ranging from taxation and expenditures, to the regulation of interstate commerce, to the declaration of war; it can also check and balance other political actors by overriding presidential vetoes, structuring the federal court system, impeaching and removing high officials, approving constitutional amendments, and in the Senate, confirming presidential appointees and ratifying treaties. Despite the enormous power of the U.S. Congress, however, it is not unusual for students of American politics to misunderstand or discount the role of Congress relative to that of the more high-profile presidency. This is in part because Congress, like most legislatures, is a large and cumbersome institution with complex structures, arcane procedures, and multiple participants. Yet to understand the nature and role of different types of legislatures, it is necessary to examine these very dimensions. As will be seen, the institutional configuration and legislative processes of the U.S. Congress offer just one of many possible types of democratic legislature, with particular implications for the functioning of American democracy.

Case Study: Legislative Variation in the Former British Dominions

Although the British Empire included many colonies, only a few countries were awarded the special, largely self-governing status of "dominions of settlement." Three of these, New Zealand, Canada, and Australia, were in regions of the world that were only sparsely populated, so they formed new societies largely transplanted from Britain. All three of these dominions chose to adopt nearly identical configurations of executive power, maintaining the British monarch (represented by a governor-general) as head of state and investing governing responsibility in a prime minister and cabinet drawn from the majority in the lower house of parliament. Strikingly, however, all three also chose rather different structures for their legislative bodies, exemplifying the three distinctive models of how a national legislature can be designed: *unicameralism, asymmetric bicameralism,* and *symmetric bicameralism.*

For several decades, New Zealand had an upper house of parliament called the Legislative Council. Because New Zealand is a unitary state with a largely homogenous population, in the 1950s it was broadly agreed that there was no compelling need for the extra layer of representation offered by the upper house and it was abolished. Since then, New Zealand has functioned well with just a single 120-member House of Representatives elected directly by the people. Occasional calls for the reinstatement of an upper house have not met with interest from the population, who feel adequately represented by a unicameral legislature, from which the prime minister and Cabinet are drawn.

Since its founding in 1867, Canada has had a bicameral parliament focused on a popularly elected House of Commons, from which the government is drawn. But unlike the case in New Zealand, the Canadian upper house, the Senate, has endured, with 105 members formally appointed by the governor-general (although actually selected by the prime minister whenever there are vacancies) for a life term up to the mandatory retirement age at 75. Senators are chosen according to a formula that draws them from all the different provinces, regions, and territories of the country, even those that are very sparsely populated.

In theory, the Canadian Senate has the same legislative powers as the Commons except that it cannot initiate bills related to revenue. Because it is an appointed body and lacks direct democratic validation, however, the Senate rarely seeks to block or even resist the will of the Commons, even when the two houses have majorities from different political parties. The Senate today generally does not initiate action but serves as a chamber of "sober second thought," offering critiques, suggestions, and amendments to bills introduced by the Commons. Free of electoral concerns, senators can offer perspectives from underrepresented groups and from the smaller provinces, and can hold open hearings to examine long-term considerations, which it did in the 1990s on the theme of euthanasia and assisted suicide. But in the end, the will of the Commons prevails, due not to written constitutional provisions but to established conventions and practices. This difference in power renders the Canadian parliament an example of asymmetric bicameralism.

Australia also maintains a bicameral parliament, but with some very significant differences. Members of the Australian Senate are elected directly by the people of the six states and two territories, with equal representation guaranteed for the six states. As a result, Senators are no less elected officials and politicians than their counterparts in the Australian House of Representatives, and they jealously guard their constitutional equality to the House in both theory and practice. The deference of the Canadian Senate to the lower house, thus, is not to be found in Australia. When the two chambers of parliament have majorities of different parties, the Senate is much more likely to stand its ground, arguing that they have as much an electoral mandate as does the House of Representatives. The relative parity of power between the two houses in Australia is an example of symmetric bicameralism.

Unicameralism

As a unitary state with all political power emanating from the national government, New Zealand is nearly a textbook case of a country that can thrive with a unicameral legislature. Without provinces or states to demand direct representation in their own right and a population that is small and fairly homogenous in terms of ethnicity, there is little need for a second chamber to represent a great diversity of interests. (One unique adaptation in New Zealand is that it provides several guaranteed seats in the House of Representatives for members of the indigenous Maori peoples.) Most countries that have unicameral legislatures are similarly unitary states with a small and fairly homogenous population; all of the Nordic countries, for instance, also practice unicameralism. However, for historical or other reasons, a significant number of unitary and/or homogenous states continue to maintain bicameral legislatures.

As might be expected, unitary states with unicameral parliamentary systems are able to act with a great deal of efficiency. Indeed, it was the fear that such legislative efficiency might lead to tyranny that was part of what prompted the American founders to subdivide Congress into two parts, creating a type of check and balance within the legislative branch. However, in countries with well-established democratic traditions, other informal political practices and independent judiciaries have helped to prevent unicameralism from leading to an abuse of power.

Unicameralism is not an entirely unknown structure in the United States. One state, Nebraska, maintains a unicameral state legislature, to no apparent detriment to the people of that (fairly low-population, fairly homogenous) state. Further, since U.S. states are unitary in nature, it is unclear how much a second state legislative chamber really adds to either the quality of representation or governance in the U.S. states, particularly in the common event when both chambers are controlled by the same political party. Many state upper houses seem to continue due to history, tradition, inertia—and to politicians who are unwilling to vote themselves out of a job. The same phenomenon appears to explain the persistence of upper houses in a number of small countries, such as a number of Caribbean island nations.

In the United States, unicameralism is also strongly the norm at the local level of government with most municipalities having a single-chambered city or town council. Even though large and diverse, New York City, in 1989, abolished its de facto upper house, which was called the Board of Estimate and represented the city's five boroughs. City and town mayors are usually directly elected by the people, although there are some municipalities that function on a quasi-parliamentary system in which the unicameral council chooses one of its own members to serve as mayor. Some U.S. municipalities even adopt a sort of head of state/head of government split, with the mayor functioning largely on a ceremonial basis and a city manager carrying out day-to-day governing.

Asymmetric Bicameralism

Among countries with parliaments, asymmetric bicameralism, as seen in the example from Canada, is the norm. This has been dubbed the "one-and-a-half" house solution: all executive and most legislative power resides in the lower house of parliament but the legitimate interests of federal units or regions are recognized through the existence of a weak upper house. Indeed, nearly all federal countries practice bicameralism and use the upper house to represent groups and interests that might otherwise be overlooked. Even a number of larger unitary states maintain upper houses to provide representation to their provinces; in France, the relatively weak upper house is even commonly called the "rural chamber" because it offers a voice for low-population, largely agricultural areas.

Unlike the case in Canada, the members of weak upper houses are generally elected, either directly by the people or by provincial legislatures. Whichever the case, members of weak upper houses understand that their positions have less power than their counterparts in the lower house. Indeed, in asymmetric bicameralism, the upper house is often a revising chamber that mostly offers divergent viewpoints and makes recommendations. Its main purpose is to add an opportunity for further deliberation and refinement of laws that might otherwise be rushed through a unicameral legislature. Weak upper houses can often influence or delay legislation but will rarely have a decisive impact when they clash with the lower house. Members of upper houses may sometimes also serve as government ministers, although rarely in major positions, and almost never as prime minister.

The two halves of the U.S. Congress were deliberately designed to be equal in power. However, to the extent that any aspect of asymmetric bicameralism can be detected in the U.S. Congress, it is actually the *upper house* that has greater powers—a distinctive feature of the U.S. Constitution (and those constitutions based on it, especially in Latin America). The U.S. Senate is constitutionally invested with two significant types of authority lacking in the U.S. House of Representatives: the confirmation of presidential appointees to high office and the ratification of international treaties. The Senate also has the final say in the impeachment process, being the sole arbiter of whether to remove an impeached president, federal judge, or other official from office. However, none of these is a specifically *legislative* power, but rather they are part of the checks-and-balances scheme of the U.S. Constitution. While the House of Representatives does have the sole right to introduce bills relating to revenue, this does not greatly enhance the power of the House because the Senate ultimately must also approve such bills.

Symmetric Bicameralism

The norm in parliamentary systems is for the lower house to be decisively more powerful than the upper house in both legislative and executive authority. Indeed, there are no countries in the world in which the government is formed solely or even primarily out of the upper house. Thus, all parliamentary systems, in terms of executive power, are asymmetric. A few parliamentary systems do, however, provide equal (although never greater) legislative power to their upper houses.

One such example, Italy, has mostly avoided clashes between the two chambers because it uses an electoral formula which all but guarantees that both houses will have the same composition in terms of political party affiliations. Australia has no such electoral formula, however, and when the two houses have majorities from different parties, it can seriously undermine the ability of the government to function. The Australian government can continue to function independently only until it needs to have a crucial piece of legislation, such as a budget. The Australian Constitution has a special provision requiring that the most serious impasses between the two houses be resolved by the drastic step of dissolving parliament, calling a national election, and then having the newly elected members of the two houses meet and vote in joint session as a single body. Given that the lower house has twice as many members as the upper house, it is almost certain to prevail. Still, this is a clumsy and difficult procedure, and in 1975 exactly such a scenario led to the country's most serious constitutional crisis. Thus, the Australian system enjoys neither the inherent stability afforded by a separation-of-powers system, nor the efficiency normally found in parliamentary systems, leading some observers to regard it as an argument against symmetric bicameralism in a parliamentary government.

By contrast, in separation-of-powers systems, symmetric bicameralism is the norm. In the United States, this separation intentionally reinforces the dispersal of power by requiring the equal consent of a majority of both houses of Congress to pass a law. In 2006, for example, comprehensive immigration reform was blocked because the two houses could not find a middle ground between a House bill focused on border enforcement and a Senate bill that would have created a guest-worker program. Further, the U.S. Senate and House of Representatives also play an equal role in the Constitutional amending process; either house may introduce an amendment and both must pass it by a two-thirds majority for it to be sent to the states. A Constitutional amendment to ban the desecration of American flag garnered two-thirds support in the House several times in the 1990s, only to be blocked repeatedly in the Senate. Similarly, symmetric powers tend to be invested in the two chambers of other national legislatures with separation-of-powers systems, such as in Latin America.

Symmetric bicameralism does not necessarily create problems for governance in the United States, but it does raise some serious issues from the perspective of democratic theory. In institutions of representative democracy, it is usually not possible to ensure that every legislator represents exactly the same number of constituents, but great pains are taken to reapportion legislative chambers periodically to address imbalances. The enormous disparities in the populations across the fifty states, however, grossly violate this proposition due to equal representation in the Senate. Of course, part of the original argument for guaranteeing two Senators for each state was to ensure the support of the less populous states, whose influence is minimal in the House, where seats are apportioned by population.

In all, upper houses whose members represent provinces, states, or regions based on geography rather than population, the potential exists for individual legislators to represent widely differing numbers of constituents. However, when upper houses are weak, this violation of the one person–one vote standard is mitigated by the subordination of the upper house to a lower house elected on the basis of population. In strong upper houses, the problem becomes clearer. In Australia, the most populous state of New South Wales has about twelve times the population of the smallest state of Tasmania, but both states have six senators. In Switzerland, the largest canton of Zurich has eighteen times the population of the smallest canton of Jura, but each has two seats in the Swiss upper house. In the United States, the disparity is far more pronounced: California has over *seventy times* more people than the least populous state of Wyoming, yet both states have two votes in the Senate.

Today, the fifty-two Senators from the twenty-six least populous states represent only about 20 percent of the U.S. population, yet they form a majority that can thwart the will of the representatives of the other 80 percent. In the United States, a small number of states representing only a tiny percentage of the population can also block a constitutional amendment, which must pass the Senate by a two-thirds majority and then be ratified by three-quarters of the states. Further, smaller states have an advantage in the Electoral College that chooses the president. This is because each state has the same number of electoral votes as it has members of Congress, in which small states are over-represented by virtue of their disproportionate number of Senate seats. In actual practice, the small-state Senators do not particularly tend to vote as a bloc: Rhode Island and Delaware have little in common with Alaska and Nebraska. Still, the U.S. Senate represents a severe distortion of the one person–one vote standard of democracy. (Ironically, the U.S. Supreme Court ruled in 1964, on the basis of the U.S. Constitution, that state and city legislatures cannot apportion their districts in ways that grossly violate the principle of one per-son–one vote. But that ruling did not affect the U.S. Senate because the rule of equal representation for the states is clearly required in Articles I and V.)

Thus, equal representation in the U.S. Senate is a classic example of a compromise made at the time of the founding that was essential for garnering support for ratification by the smaller states. The argument for equal representation of the states was questionable even at the time of the founding, but the emergence of a strong national identity, mobility across states, stronger linkages via mass media, and many other factors make it profoundly anachronistic today. Although Senate equal representation is widely considered unalterable, it would theoretically be possible to move toward a system of asymmetric bicameralism by passing a Constitutional amendment to weaken the powers of the Senate to make it into more of a revising chamber, per-haps by giving the House the power to override it by a two-thirds vote. Such a change remains a practical impossibility, however, precisely because any such amendment would require the support of many of the smaller states whose power would be diluted.

The Dispersal of Power in the U.S. Congress

By their very nature, separation-of-powers systems lead to the dis-persal of power across three branches of government. This dispersal is further increased by bicameralism, and particularly symmetric bicam-eralism, in which the equal consent of both houses is required to pass legislation. But power in the U.S. Congress is even further dispersed because of the very limited control of the political parties over indi-vidual members and because of the powerful role played by congres-sional committees.

Relative to legislators in other countries, members of Congress have an exceptional degree of autonomy from their party leaders. One major reason for this is because the leadership of political parties in the United States do not simply choose their own party nominees in elections, as is the case in many other countries. Rather, the system of primary elections means that elected officials must win the support of the registered voters of their party rather than the party's leaders.

While political parties can offer, or withhold, considerable monetary and other resources, candidates for office must ultimately prioritize the needs and wishes of their constituents rather than their parties. In parliamentary systems, the power of party leaders is also strengthened by their ability to determine which backbenchers will be promoted through the ranks of parliament to ministerial office. Thus, parliamentarians who resist their party leaders run the risk of not only losing renomination in the next election but the loss of any upward mobility within government. By contrast, American politicians who aspire to higher office are largely on their own and may even find electoral advantages to distinguishing themselves from their party's leadership.

Thus, members of the U.S. Congress can and do routinely vote against their own party leaders in ways that members of parliaments rarely do. The only time that there is a rigid norm requiring members of Congress to support their parties is after each election, when a vote is taken to determine which party has a majority and thus will be in control of the leadership of each chamber and of all committees. In practice, however, members of the same party in the U.S. Congress do tend to vote together in large numbers, in part because of broad ideological agreement within parties, and in part because individual members may calculate that it is in their own interest for their party to succeed. It also reflects that party leaders in Congress know better than to not bring a bill up for a vote until they are assured of broad agreement within the party, thus keeping dissension behind closed doors rather than revealing it in open votes.

The weakness of party leadership is most pronounced in the Senate, where the rules of debate mean that each individual can threaten a filibuster. To a degree that is astonishing when viewed in comparative perspective, any single U.S. Senator—not just party leaders or even just members of the majority—wields an enormous ability to influence and obstruct the passage of legislation by means of a filibuster threat. Further, the requirement that sixty Senators vote for cloture in order to end a filibuster further extends power to the minority party. Thus, it is not unusual for a bill to pass the House by a simple majority and to have the support of fifty-one Senators but still fail to be passed because a filibuster prevented the Senate from taking a vote. Exactly such an eventuality occurred during the first attempts in early 2007 to pass a congressional resolution opposing President Bush's plans for a surge in the number of troops posted in Iraq.

By contrast, in the House, tighter procedural rules make that chamber more like a parliament. Still, the speaker and other leaders of the majority party are not able to simply ram through their own agendas, and sometimes must modify their goals in order to ensure majority support. Such an active role for individual rank-and-file legislators is almost unheard of in the world; unlike most members of national legislatures, members of the U.S. Congress genuinely do play a fundamentally important role in the governance of the country.

Individual members of Congress also have an enhanced degree of autonomy because they are given their own fairly extensive staffs and offices, in both Washington, D.C. and in their constituencies. Membership in Congress is a full-time job with commensurate pay, in contrast to legislatures in which those who do not serve in government positions or in legislative leadership roles maintain outside careers and work only part time. The resources, and professional time, available to members of Congress enable them to provide services directly to voters, such as intervening on their behalf when they are having problems with some part of the government bureaucracy. Such constituency service has little or no bearing on the legislative duties of members of Congress but enables them to enhance their likelihood of reelection, thus further reinforcing their individual autonomy. This is, however, also another manifestation of the commonly cited concern that members of Congress must spend so much of their time on reelection activities that they have inadequate time and energy to actually be effective legislators.

Power is also dispersed in Congress because of the strength of the committee system. Most legislatures employ a committee structure because of the practical benefits it provides, such as division of labor and specialization, that enable individual bills to be assigned for closer scrutiny and amendment to standing committees. No legislative chamber can, as a whole, address all the issues that come before it with anything near the attention to detail or expert knowledge that committee structures allow. What is unusual in the U.S. Congress is the high degree of participation in the process enjoyed by committees, which allows multiple players to have direct input into the shape of legislation.

Indeed, only about 10 percent of bills that are proposed in the U.S. Congress ever become law, in large part because there are so many points at which a bill can be stopped during the process. Whereas committees in many legislatures play an advisory role, congressional committees can make or break a bill. It is a very common occurrence for a bill to "die in committee" either because powerful committee chairs choose not to allow it to come up for a vote or because it is defeated in a vote of committee members. While there are some procedures for getting around the committee structure that can be invoked by each chamber's leadership or membership as a whole, these are cumbersome and seldom used.

Not only are congressional committees important for determining which bills will or will not make it to the floor of each chamber for a vote, but they also play a major role in shaping the substance of the bill. By holding public hearings, conducting mark ups, and taking various other actions, committees play a major role in determining the scope and provisions of bills. Additional changes can be made by the leaders of each chamber, and sometimes also by amendment by the members of the chamber, especially in the Senate. While members of the majority party usually have more opportunities for input, the voices of members of the minority party tend to be heeded rather more than in parliamentary systems where they are relegated to the role of opposition.

For a bill to become a law, in summary, it must pass through an extraordinary number of hurdles in the U.S. system. These include, but are not limited to, the chairs and memberships of at least one subcommittee and one committee in each house, the leadership and the memberships of both houses, a conference committee to iron out differences between the House and Senate versions, and the president. This complicated procedure has been cited as an inertial force in U.S. politics, making it difficult to change the status quo or tackle new problems quickly or efficiently. Whereas the loyalty of members of Congress to their individual districts or states may make them better representatives in a narrow sense, this also obstructs the development of coherent national legislative agendas.

Certainly, the legislative process in the U.S. Congress is infinitely more complicated than in those parliamentary systems where the government is essentially assured that any bill it proposes will quickly and easily pass into law. This is not to say that parliamentary party leaders are free to completely disregard the wishes of their backbenchers, or even that they would wish to do so. Government ministers can benefit from the constructive input of rank-and-file members of parliament and try to avoid debates in parliament or anonymous comments in the press that might cast the work of the government in a bad light. However, when push comes to shove, the executives in parliamentary systems can almost always get their way over the legislature.

The Power of Congress in Comparative Perspective

The dispersal of power in the U.S. Congress across houses, committees, and individual members should not detract attention from the fact that the U.S. Congress still exercises a great deal of power—far more than most other legislatures. Indeed, there is not even much point in examining the legislative role in nondemocratic countries because such legislatures are likely to be simply rubber stamps for laws submitted from the executive, offering a veil of legitimacy for executive actions. At most, they may serve in a nonbinding advisory capacity, perhaps sometimes offer constructive ideas and technical expertise in the crafting of the laws, but ultimately being completely dominated by the executive.

Even in democratic countries, legislatures sometimes play only secondary roles. In parliamentary systems, legislative majorities are the ultimate source of, and check on, executive authority because the prime minister must maintain the confidence of a majority to continue in office. The power to bring down the executive through a vote of no confidence, or by replacing a party leader, is the ultimate power that is invested in parliaments but denied to Congress, as discussed in Chapter 4. However, once a solid parliamentary government has been formed, most of the legislative initiative usually comes from government ministers.

The U.S. Congress, on the other hand, really is a coequal branch of government. In the United States, presidents certainly can and do propose legislation, but such proposals represent only starting points in the process. And although presidents can veto laws (subject to a congressional override), they cannot prevent Congress from taking up any issue it wishes, nor can they force Congress to pass a law against its will. Even after a bill is authorized, Congress must also vote to appropriate funds because many laws are meaningless without access to the funding needed to implement and administer them. Presidents may take the initiative to introduce a budget but know that it will be substantially altered by Congress in exercise of its power of the purse. This authority also gives Congress formidable leverage over the federal bureaucracy, which is closely overseen by committees in both houses.

In theory, separation of powers can also help to enhance the role of national legislatures in other presidential systems, especially throughout Latin America. But most such countries still tend to be more heavily president-centered. Constitutionally, many Latin American presidents have more far-reaching powers than the American president. Some, for instance, have a line item veto, which enables them to pick and choose which parts of bills they wish to sign into law (some U.S. state governors have this power, but the president does not). More importantly, many Latin American presidents have—whether legally or extra-legally—the ability to declare a state of emergency and to rule directly by presidential decree, backed by their control of police and military forces. In the 1970s and 1980s, nearly every country in South America experienced direct rule by a president supported by, or sometimes manipulated by, the military.

In many of these cases, presidents squared off directly against legislatures, with the latter almost invariably proving to be the losers. As recently as 1992, President Alberto Fujimori of Peru used his control of the military, amid economic crisis and threats from the Shining Path guerilla fighters, to forcibly disband both houses of the Peruvian congress. When he came under international pressure, Fujimori called new elections for a congress only one third the size of its predecessor and used his control over the electoral process to ensure that the new congress would be filled with his supporters. The new congress then, obligingly, amended the Constitution to strengthen the formal powers of the president and to allow multiple terms of office. In some other cases, Latin American presidents have dominated their political systems not explicitly through the use of force, but by suppressing opposition parties and factions. In perhaps the clearest example, for nearly seventy years Mexican presidents totally dominated the Congress due to the near-monopoly of the ruling Revolutionary Institutional Party. The Mexican Congress was reduced largely to a consultative and technical role rather than that of a coequal branch of government.

Emphasizing the power of the U.S. Congress does not in any way derogate the tremendous power of U.S. presidents, which has grown considerably since the 1930s due to the larger role of the executive branch of the federal government and the increased focus on military and foreign affairs. Unlike prime ministers, U.S. presidents can at times act unilaterally, either on the basis of their own constitutional powers or on the basis of power delegated to the executive in laws passed earlier by Congress. Indeed, the administration of President George W. Bush has been especially aggressive in expanding the scope of presidential power and curbing the role of Congress. During the first six years of his presidency, at least one house, and usually both houses, of Congress was under the control of Republicans who were glad to follow Bush's lead and rarely questioned his power. In the aftermath of the September 11, 2001, terrorist attacks, Congress quickly passed laws such as the USA PATRIOT Act expanding the executive's power to detect and prosecute terrorism-related crimes. In 2003, Congress also authorized the president to invade Iraq based, among other reasons, on the threat that Saddam Hussein possessed weapons of mass destruction.

The early 2000s represented the greatest ebb of congressional independence in decades, making it in some ways similar to the model of ineffectual Latin American legislatures who follow the lead of their president. But by 2006, Congress and the public learned that the U.S. military had been using torture and depriving detainees of due process rights in Iraq and elsewhere, and that Iraq had not, in fact, possessed weapons of mass destruction. Likewise, press reports revealed that the president had authorized the wire-tapping of phones within the United States without obtaining judicial warrants, as required by the Fourth Amendment. Against a backdrop of a failed military and foreign policy in Iraq and the catastrophic inability of the federal government to respond to the Hurricane Katrina disaster of 2005, Congress began reasserting itself. After Democrats gained control of both houses in the 2006 elections, Congress was poised to once again assume a major autonomous role in governing the country.

Conclusion

Perhaps more than any other national legislature in the world, the U.S. Congress not only represents the people but also plays an active role in the governance of the country. Unlike parliaments, the U.S. Congress is not subject to direction by the executive branch; unlike the congresses in other separation-of-powers systems, it has managed to hold its own against the power of the sword wielded by presidents. Yet, if the power of Congress is enormous, it is also dispersed between two houses of equal authority, across a network of influential committees and subcommittees, and ultimately among the elected members themselves. And Congress is ultimately subject to the constitutional structure of checks and balances through means such as the presidential veto and, as will be discussed at greater length in the next chapter, the judicial review of the federal court system.

Further Reading

- *Legislatures: Comparative Perspectives on Representative Assemblies.* Gerhard Loewenberg, Peverill Squire, and D. Roderick Kiewiet, Eds. The University of Michigan Press, Ann Arbor: 2002.
- *Legislatures and Legislators.* Philip Norton, Ed. Ashgate, Brookfield, VT: 1998.
- *Democratic Legislative Institutions: A Comparative View.* David M. Olson. M.E. Sharpe, Armonk, New York: 1994.

Web-Based Exploration Exercise

Visit the Web site for U.S. the House of Representatives (<www.house.gov>). Then use the parliamentary Web page of the Inter-Parliamentary Union (<www.ipu.org/english/parlweb.htm>) to visit the Web site of the *lower* houses of at least two other legislatures. Identify at least one similarity and one difference that you find with regard to the role of that house in the passage of a bill into a law.

Question for Debate and Discussion

One of the major hallmarks of the U.S. Congress is the way power is dispersed among both houses, multiple committees, and even among the members. How could power be consolidated in Congress in order to make it more like a parliament? Would this be desirable? What would be the disadvantages of a concentration of power in the hands of a few leaders?

7

THE JUDICIAL BRANCH

The Supreme Court and the Federal Courts

While executive and legislative branches are always indisputably political, the judicial branch of government is often viewed as quite separate and distinct from politics and also less notably powerful than the other branches. Executives have the power of the sword, the ability to use force to achieve their goals, while many legislatures have the power of the purse, the ability to choose how funds are allocated. Denied these two sources of power and removed from day-to-day politics, judiciaries are generally a distant third force in government. In the famous words of Alexander Hamilton, the judiciary is "the least dangerous branch" in terms of its ability to dominate a political system or tyrannize the people. Still, the Supreme Court is a major player in American politics, and in political systems throughout the world, courts are playing an increasingly autonomous and influential role.

Judiciaries vary enormously from country to country, even more so than do executive and legislative structures. The role they play also extends beyond the realm of politics into such areas as criminal justice, contracts, land use, family law, and many other areas that are beyond the scope of this book. To assess the political role of the judiciary in any country, and to serve as a basis of comparison for the U.S. judiciary, there are three major questions to consider: Are the courts impartial and independent? Are they a separate and coequal, or a subordinate, branch of government? Do they have the power of judicial review—the ability to strike down executive and legislative acts that conflict with a nation's constitution? As might be expected, in nondemocratic countries, the answer to all of these questions would be no. And the answer to all three of those questions in the United States is an emphatic yes. But to a degree that might surprise many Americans, there are many democratic countries in which the answers to these questions are rather less clear cut.

Case Study: The Judiciary in France

To an even greater degree than in the United States, the government and politics of France are defined by its revolutionary tradition. Historically, judges in France had been viewed as agents of the king, and they were thus on the losing side of the French Revolution of 1789. In an attempt to rationalize legal proceedings and ensure the authority of the state, detailed legal codes were promulgated by Napoleon in the early nineteenth century, and then exported throughout the European continent both by his armies and by the force of his example. Ever since, courts in France, and throughout continental Europe, have remained subordinate to—indeed almost extensions of—the executive and legislative branches.

Today in France, law courts are viewed as administrative organs of the state, playing more of a supporting role than acting as an independent force. Judges are civil servants, some directly employed by the Ministry of Justice, and are expected more to assist the executive in enforcing the law than to uphold or protect the rights of individuals or the society at large. In cases of criminal prosecution, for instance, the principal task of judges is to help to determine the guilt or innocence of the accused rather than acting, as in the United States, as impartial referees in an adversarial confrontation between a prosecutor and a defendant. French courts also have no right to strike down actions taken by the executive branch of government. This power is reserved to a semiautonomous body set up *within* the executive branch called the Council of State, assisted by a system of subordinate administrative courts that hear complaints against the bureaucracy.

Limits on the French judiciary do not stop there. The development of highly detailed legal statutes beginning with the Napoleonic Code means that courts in France are required to rule on particular cases as narrowly as possible. While the ruling of judges is binding in the specific case before them, it does not establish precedent and generally cannot be cited when similar issues arise in other cases. French courts also lack the ability to strike down laws as being unconstitutional. That task is assigned to a quasi-independent Constitutional Council that can be called upon to determine the constitutionality of laws, although only after they have been passed by parliament and before they have been signed into law by the president. The Constitutional Council, which has become more active in recent decades, is not a court but a political body appointed jointly by the President and the heads of the two chambers of the national legislature.

As befits a unitary state, France has a single unified court system, rather than multiple court systems in each of its provinces. Within the judicial system, cases can be appealed up to the highest judicial body, the Court of Cassation, which may review cases from all lower courts. The Court does not decide cases itself but can remand them for retrial to a different lower court than the one from which a case originated. Strikingly, the newly designated lower court is generally *not* bound by the findings of the Court, which itself consists of dozens of judges fragmented into multiple panels dealing with different cases and rarely capable of coordinated action as a single entity. By no means is the Court of Cassation analogous to the U.S. Supreme Court, nor can the French judiciary play anything like the role of the U.S. federal courts.

Impartiality and Independence

The idea that courts must act impartially is a long-standing principle of democratic politics; in a country in which all people are equal, the law should apply to all people equally. Yet in practice, the line separating courts in nondemocratic and democratic systems may not always be so clear. Indeed, in the vast majority of cases that have no political implications, courts in nondemocratic countries may be perfectly capable of applying existing legal norms to routine issues such as traffic violations, contract disputes, divorce settlements, or personal assaults. The relevant line of division in such cases may well be not whether a country is democratic, but the degree to which its judges and court personnel are susceptible to bribery or are vulnerable to threats of violent retaliation. Thus in cases with no political implications, the legal system in a nondemocratic but fairly capably governed country such as China may well be more impartial than that in a more democratic but less well-governed country such as Brazil.

On the whole, the courts in long-established democracies perform with the greatest impartiality and professionalism, but the correlation is inexact and certainly no system is entirely free of bias and corruption. Further, in countries such as the United States where judges tend to play the role of neutral arbiters, differences in wealth and education can become greatly magnified. This is because a greater burden falls on individual defendants who may lack the educational background to assist in their own defense or the economic means to hire highly qualified legal representation. In systems in which judges play a more active role, the quality of the defense becomes a less crucial factor.

The question of the independence of the courts is always relevant when a case has political implications. Such implications may arise when a case involves someone powerful or well connected, for instance, when a wealthy contributor to a political party or public official is charged with business fraud. Political implications may also develop when a case involves actions by government, such as adjudicating whether police officers used excessive force against protestors. In cases with political implications, a well-timed phone call to a judge, whether to exert pressure or make an overt threat, may be all that is needed to ensure a favorable outcome. In some countries, deference to the powerful may even be so thoroughly ingrained that no such call is even needed; judges simply know how they must rule to preserve their personal and professional well being.

The court system in the United States is generally considered both impartial and independent. A major source of independence among federal judges, including Supreme Court justices, is that once nominated by the president and confirmed by the Senate, their terms extend for life or until they decide to retire (the possibility of impeachment by Congress also exists, but is exceedingly unlikely). Federal judges thus have no further accountability to the executive or the legislative branches and are largely free from the pressures of public opinion or concerns about reelection. However, many state, county, and municipal judges are elected, making them more similar to politicians. And even federal judges, because of the significant political role of the courts, are often initially chosen by presidents for their ideological views as much as their legal skills. In countries where the courts play a narrower role, judges are more likely to be selected for their technical competence and experience.

Courts as a Separate and Co-Equal Branch

Even when courts are both impartial and independent, it need not be the case that they are considered a completely separate and coequal branch of government. As seen in the case of France, courts in some democratic countries—indeed throughout most of the countries of continental Europe and in their former colonies abroad—may be viewed as organs of the state with an important but narrow technical role. In fact, France is the prototype of a civil law system in which legislation is spelled out in great detail and specificity at the time that it is written by the legislature. The principal source of the meaning of law is the wording of the statutes as written by the legislature and, to a lesser extent, their explication in analyses by law professors. Prior rulings by other judges carry little weight because the codified laws are considered to contain all the answers that a judge needs to rule on any specific case.

This approach contrasts sharply with the common law system that prevails in Britain and in many former British colonies, including the United States. In common law systems, laws tend to be fewer in number and written with less detail. As cases arise, judges have much greater discretion to articulate the broader meaning of the law, indeed helping to write the law in some senses. Their rulings establish case law that establishes precedent that can and must be cited when similar situations arise in future cases. Lower courts are bound by the rulings of higher courts, and even the Supreme Court tends to apply the principle of *stare decisis* ("let the decision stand") under which precedent should not be overturned without very compelling reasons.

In recent decades, the two systems have converged to some degree, with civil law judges becoming more likely to cite previous cases and legislatures in common law countries producing more detailed codification of laws. And even in common law systems, the extent to which judges should play a role in creating law remains controversial. Since the 1970s, and very sharply more recently, there has been widespread criticism in the United States of "legislating from the bench" by judicial activists. Such critics, who tend to be from the conservative side of the political spectrum, feel that judges have in recent decades exceeded the scope of their roles by making expansive rulings, especially in the area of civil liberties and civil rights. These critics instead endorse the idea of deference to original intent. Under this concept, judges are bound to interpret laws in light of what was intended by the legislature that first passed such laws, be it Congress for federal law, a state legislature for state law, or the framers of 1787 in the case of the U.S. Constitution. This approach would move the U.S. judiciary closer to a civil law system and weaken the ability of courts to be independent actors in the political system. Those preferring a more flexible system with a greater role for judges generally argue that the Constitution and the law should be interpreted as living documents whose meanings evolve over time and whose broad principles must be adapted to changing circumstances.

Another distinction between civil law and common law systems also profoundly affects the role of judges. In common law countries, an adversarial approach is employed in which judges act essentially as neutral arbiters standing between two parties and ensuring that proper legal procedures are employed. In criminal cases, in which a person is charged with breaking a law, those two parties would be the prosecutor and the accused, the prosecutor bearing the burden to demonstrate beyond a reasonable doubt the guilt of the accused, who is presumed innocent until proven guilty. (Civil cases, in which one person claims to have been economically harmed by another, are of less interest for present purposes because they involve action by private parties rather than by government.) In common law countries, and especially in the United States, the role of the judge is even further limited by the use of juries composed of ordinary citizens to determine the guilt or innocence of the accused.

In civil law systems, the role of the judge is very different. Rather than using an adversarial approach, civil law systems tend to employ the inquisitorial approach in which the goal is not for one side or the other to win the case, but to find the objective truth in a situation. Before the start of an inquisitorial trial, an entire investigation has been conducted by a different judge to determine whether the case should even come to trial. If this high threshold has been met, then it is considered that the accused is quite unlikely to be completely innocent (although this should not give rise to an outright presumption of guilt.) The goal of the judge in such an inquisitorial approach then is not to be a neutral arbiter between parties, but to actively engage in the questioning process and to seek to resolve the question before the court. Thus in criminal trials in civil law systems, judges do not stand between the government and the accused, but rather work on behalf of the government to determine whether the accused is guilty.

Judicial Review

As can be seen from this discussion, judges in common law systems constitute a branch of government that is separate and coequal in that courts are not simply vehicles for propounding the intentions of legislators or of advancing the law enforcement goals of executives. But in the United States, the federal courts also have the authority to strike down actions by Congress, the president, or the states that they deem to be unconstitutional. Although the nature and scope of judicial review is not explicitly included in the wording of the U.S. Constitution, it was established by the 1803 case of *Marbury v. Madison* and has been widely accepted ever since. (State supreme courts also have the final say over the meaning of their respective state constitutions.)

Judicial review is fairly uncontroversial as it applies to the power of higher courts to review the rulings of lower courts. It is also understood that in a federal system, the highest national court must be able to overrule the courts of the provinces, states, or other federal units, at least on issues that involve federal questions. More controversial, however, is that federal courts can and do strike down laws passed by Congress which violate some principle of the Constitution. For instance, in the 1996 *Lopez* case, the Supreme Court ruled that Congress exceeded its power under the Interstate Commerce Clause by banning guns in schools that are administered by the states. In the

2006 *Hamdan* case, the Supreme Court specifically rejected the Bush administration's use of military tribunals to try terrorism suspects.

Although such cases of overt judicial review are not very common, the will of the Supreme Court does sometimes trump that of the legislative and executive branches, serving as a major source of checks and balances. Indeed, the powerful role of the U.S. Supreme Court is a significant factor in explaining why the separation-of-powers system that has contributed to so many dictatorial presidents in Latin America has not done so in the United States. The institutional prestige of the Supreme Court has, for example, permitted it to intervene at two pivotal moments in recent political history when a constitutional crisis loomed. In 1974 during the Watergate affair, the Supreme Court broke a deadlock between Congress and President Richard Nixon over release of taped conversations made in the Oval Office, setting off a chain of events that led to Nixon's resignation. In 2000, with the outcome of the presidential election deadlocked in Florida, the Supreme Court stepped in with a ruling that effectively allocated the state's electoral votes to George W. Bush. In his concession speech, Al Gore accepted the ruling even as he signaled his disagreement with it. Without a Supreme Court capable of rendering an authoritative decision in these cases, American democracy might well have been threatened.

By comparison, Supreme Courts in less established democracies rarely have the same degree of authority, either tending to provide a justification for the outcome preferred by those in power or finding their rulings ignored (and perhaps their jobs and even their lives imperiled). Even robustly democratic countries, however, vary in the degree of judicial review that they afford their courts. At one end is Britain, where the tradition of parliamentary supremacy means that the House of Commons is free to set aside any court ruling it wishes and cannot be bound or overruled by the judiciary. This reality has traditionally been underscored by the rather odd institutional placement of the nation's highest court as a separate body within the House of Lords (although this is due to change in October 2008 with the establishment of a separate supreme court). In recent years, British membership in the European Union (EU) has begun to complicate matters, because the parliaments of all member countries of the EU are subject to judicial review by some EU courts. This remains an evolving issue but, for the first time in centuries, the concept of definitive judicial review is gaining ground on long-standing European traditions of parliamentary supremacy.

Canada has a unique twist on the issue of judicial review, giving its Supreme Court full powers of judicial review over federal and provincial parliaments in its 1982 constitution. However, due to objections from some provinces, the Canadian Constitution includes the so-called "Notwithstanding Clause." This provision allows the Supreme Court to make a ruling, but empowers the federal or any provincial parliament to reassert a law "notwithstanding" the view of the Supreme Court that it violates the Canadian Charter of Rights and Freedoms. Such assertion of parliamentary supremacy has never been used at the federal level, although the province of Quebec asserted it twice to uphold laws favoring the use of French even after the Supreme Court ruled that both French and English have equal status. Despite the sparse use of the Notwithstanding Clause, its very existence undoubtedly restrains the Canadian Supreme Court in ways that the U.S. Supreme Court is not restrained.

As we have seen, France does not allow its courts any degree of influence in reviewing the constitutionality of executive or legislative acts; several neighboring countries such as Belgium and the Netherlands have similar systems. A number of other European countries, including Italy, Austria, and Germany, have established special constitutional courts with powers of judicial review. However, these constitutional courts as well as those in many less well-established democracies in Eastern Europe, the former Soviet Union, and elsewhere, can be difficult for citizens to access and often have limits on the issues they can address. Also, in these countries, only the official constitutional court can rule on constitutional issues, whereas in the United States all federal courts have this authority, with the Supreme Court having final say. Thus, judicial review can be, and is, applied by dozens of courts throughout the United States on a regular basis, greatly expanding its use and scope.

Perhaps the most significant exercise of judicial review in the United States during the twentieth century was *Brown v. Board of Education*. Between 1896 and 1954, the brutal system of racial segregation that prevailed in the American South had the full endorsement of the Supreme Court under the theory that the equal protection clause of the Fourteenth Amendment permitted separate facilities for whites and blacks as long as they were equal. In practice, though, equal provisions could be stretched to mean that blacks and whites were treated equally if both had access to schools, even if the black schools had untrained teachers, inadequate supplies, and poorly maintained buildings. In *Brown*, the Supreme Court recognized the reality that "separate is inherently unequal," opening the floodgates for a half century of social advances for minority and disadvantaged groups.

Despite some reservations, U.S. presidents from Eisenhower to Kennedy to Johnson took the ruling seriously enough to deploy federal forces to back up desegregation orders. Congress eventually also came around by passing the Civil Rights Act of 1964 to enforce the Fourteenth Amendment and the Voting Rights Act of 1965 to fulfill the Fifteenth Amendment's promise that race would not be a barrier to full citizenship. During the same era, the Supreme Court also redefined the scope of the Bill of Rights, vigorously reinforcing freedom of speech and the press, proactively protecting the rights of the criminals and accused, and articulating a right to privacy in areas of sexuality and reproduction.

The power of judicial review not only is significant for the system of checks and balances in the United States, but also has implications for political participation. In many countries, there is little if any hope of effecting significant political change through the court system because courts either have limited power or are difficult to access for ordinary people. In the United States, the federal courts are a major point of access into the political system, one that is especially important for minority groups that are unlikely to be able to achieve their aims through the electoral process. Because the federal courts are entrusted with the authority to protect constitutionally established civil liberties and civil rights regardless of the will of the majority, minority groups have found it particularly effective to use the court system to advance their cause. However, this trend has gone some way toward reinforcing a popular antipathy in some circles toward unelected, unaccountable judges who are seen as imposing their own views rather than merely interpreting the law.

Despite its enormous powers, the U.S. Supreme Court does labor under a number of limitations. One restraint is that its jurisdiction is limited to actual cases and controversies, and can be altered by act of Congress. Unlike constitutional courts in many other countries, the U.S. Supreme Court cannot issue advisory opinions in the abstract about whether a particular law would pass constitutional muster. Instead, it must wait for a law to be enacted, challenged in lower courts, and eventually appealed up to the Supreme Court. Then it must find a place for it on its extremely limited docket of cases. The Supreme Court rejects some 99% of the appeals that are made to it, meaning that many constitutional questions are ultimately decided by lower courts. Thus, the theoretical power of the U.S. Supreme Court to exercise judicial review is limited by its capacity as an institution, although it is generally still free to choose the cases it deems most significant. Further, the limited institutional capacity of the Supreme Court does not diminish the judiciary's overall power of judicial review as much as it disperses that power widely throughout the federal court system as a whole.

The courts also face the reality that their rulings are not self-executing, but rather must be carried out by Congress, the president, the bureaucracy, or in some cases, the states. Thus, courts must exercise a certain degree of self-restraint, issuing rulings that are as persuasive as possible and that do not too sharply overstep the bounds of what the public or other political actors will be willing to accept and enact. For example, the expansive and historic ruling in *Brown* was followed by a much more tempered requirement that desegregation be carried out with all deliberate speed rather than on a fixed timetable. It then took until 1971 before the courts ordered more vigorous enforcement of racial integration through compulsory busing of students to achieve racial balance in primary schools. The subsequent history of integration efforts also reveals much about the limits of judicial power. It has largely succeeded in areas such as employment and access to public accommodations such as theaters, restaurants, and hotels. However, it has in many ways failed in housing and primary education, with minorities almost as segregated de facto today as they were under law fifty years ago. The courts in the United States play an extraordinarily important role, but they are but one of many political players and are far from the judicial tyrants that some have accused them of being.

Conclusion

No other country invests it court system with the scale and scope of power that the United States does. Still, the role of the judiciary has been expanding throughout the world, exercising more vigorous powers of judicial review. This can have a very salutary effect on democracy, particularly when it reins in dictatorial executives and protects individual civil liberties. But it is unlikely that the U.S. court system could be successfully transplanted in full to other countries. Indeed, it remains one of the remarkable factors of American democracy that the two elected branches do not more often disregard Supreme Court rulings with which they disagree. This is in part due to the self-restraint exercised by the Court in not overreaching in the scope and timing of its rulings. But such deference is also due to a particular reverence for the U.S. Constitution as being virtually synonymous with the state itself. Neither of these factors can simply be created out of thin air in other countries, which may have very different political histories and cultures.

Further Reading

- *The Judicial Process: An Introductory Analysis of the Courts of the United States, England and France.* Henry J. Abraham. Oxford University Press, New York: 1993.
- *Courts, Laws, and Politics in Comparative Perspective.* Herbert Jacob et al. Yale University Press, New Haven, CT: 1996.

Web-Based Exploration Exercise

Visit the Web site of the Supreme Court of another country and examine the structure of that court and of that country's judicial system. Identify at least one similarity and one difference with the U.S. system and discuss their implications for functioning of the judiciary.

A comprehensive portal to the world's supreme courts can be found at <www.globalcourts.com/mini-oversikt.html>. The U.S. Supreme Court's Web site can be accessed at <www.supremecourtus.gov>.

Question for Debate and Discussion

In many ways, the U.S. Supreme Court is the most powerful court of law in the world. Given that judges are unelected and serve life terms, should the expansive powers of the judiciary be curbed? Based on the models of other countries, how could the U.S. Supreme Court be reined in? What would be the advantages and disadvantages of such a change?

III

POLITICAL
PARTICIPATION

8

VOTING AND ELECTIONS

Voting and elections are an absolute prerequisite for democracy, the very definition of which is "rule by the people." *Direct* democracy, which refers to the practice of having the people vote directly on all matters of importance, is now extremely rare in the world. Only a handful of jurisdictions—and none at the national level—are still small and uncomplicated enough to allow for direct democracy. *Representative* democracy, by far the predominant form of democracy today, involves the election of individuals to public offices in which they are empowered to exercise authority on behalf of the people.

In order for a country to qualify as a bona fide democracy, elections must be free, fair, and competitive, and the right to vote and to run for office should be open to all, or nearly all, adult citizens. Beyond basic questions of electoral procedure and broad citizen participation, however, systems of voting and elections diverge greatly across democratic countries. Some countries place a very light burden on their voters, with elections being held only every few years and with a limited number of offices to fill. Others, perhaps most prominently the United States, have frequent elections with quite complicated ballots. Many countries facilitate the participation of their citizens in elections; others—including the United States—take a less proactive approach, leaving it mostly up to citizens' own initiative with the predictable result of low voter turnout. Finally, the particular electoral system used can determine how votes are translated into seats, and whether only the will of the majority prevails or election outcomes reflect the wishes of a larger portion of the electorate.

Case Study: Voting and Elections in Israel

Israel has a robust, even combative democracy, but in many ways, Israeli voting and elections are far more straightforward and streamlined than in the United States. This geographically tiny country is a unitary state, meaning that there are no levels of government between the local and the national for which elections must be held. It also employs a parliamentary system with just a single chamber, the Knesset, which in turn elects both the prime minister and a ceremonial president. Further, there are no electoral districts—all 120 seats of the Knesset are filled by a single national election. Essentially, then, Israelis must answer only a single question when they go to the voting booth in national elections: which party do they wish to support for power?

This question may sounds like an easy one to most Americans, being used to a two-party system, or even to many Europeans accustomed to having perhaps four or five parties. But in Israel, the political party system is highly fragmented along ideological, religious, and ethnic lines, with more than a dozen political parties contesting each election. Under Israeli election rules, each party gets the same percentage of seats as the percentage of the national vote that it wins (a system called proportional representation [PR]). The only limitation is that the party must receive at least 2 percent of the national vote to be apportioned any seats. In elections held in March 2006, the two largest parties were the centrist Kadima Party with 22 percent of the vote and 29 seats and the left-wing Labour Party with 15 percent of the vote and 19 seats. But twelve parties in total received more than 2 percent of the vote and thus at least three seats in the Knesset. This level of multiparty fragmentation is so commonplace that no single party in Israel's more than fifty-year history has ever been able to establish a majority in the Knesset: all Israeli governments have been based on coalitions among multiple parties.

As for electoral law, all Israeli citizens over the age of eighteen are eligible to vote, including the significant number of Arabs and other non-Jews who are citizens. In order to facilitate wide-scale participation, election day is a national holiday and special arrangements are made for active duty soldiers, overseas diplomats, the hospital-bound, and even prisoners to cast a ballot. Voter turnout routinely reaches the 80 percent mark, although it dropped to 63 percent in 2006 because of an unusually confused political situation.

The picture of democracy and electoral participation in Israel is complicated, of course, by the long-term Israeli occupation of Palestinian territories. The residents of the West Bank and the Gaza Strip are heavily influenced by the policies chosen by Israeli elected officials, but have no say in those elections. However, in recent years they have had their own elections for the government of the Palestinian Authority.

Free and Fair Elections

As stated above, a minimal criterion for democracy is that elections must be free, fair, and competitive. Free elections require secret ballots and protection from coercion in how individuals vote. In the past in the United States (and still in some countries today), voters had to publicly request a color-coded ballot for one party slate or another when at the voting booth. This choice could then be recorded, and voters would often be in plain sight when carrying and casting their votes, the color of their ballot clearly visible. Whenever the secrecy of the ballot is compromised, individuals can be subjected to enormous pressure to vote a certain way from family members, communities, employers, or the government itself. In the United States today, as in most democratic countries, the use of secret ballots, usually in a curtained or otherwise isolated voting booth, largely removes such problems (although they are being considered anew in the context of proposals to expand voting by mail and/or via the Internet).

The question of whether elections are fair raises a different set of concerns, which secret balloting can do nothing to ensure. Guaranteeing the fairness of an election rests almost entirely with the authorities who oversee elections to ensure that strict procedures are adhered to. Yet the United States has an extraordinarily decentralized, even chaotic, system for administering elections. Unlike voting rights, which are largely regulated at the national level, elections are explicitly designated in the Constitution as a right and responsibility of the states. Indeed, there is no such thing as a national election in the United

States—even the presidential election is really fifty-one separate elections, in each of the states and in the District of Columbia. Further, many states devolve much of the responsibility for administering elections to the county level, meaning that there are thousands of different policies and procedures in place throughout the United States. By contrast, centralized control of voting procedures allows fewer opportunities for fraud, although it by no means prevents it entirely. In one infamous incident in 1988, for instance, the central government computers being used to tabulate the results of the overall presidential election in Mexico mysteriously crashed when the opposition candidate pulled ahead. When they were operational again, the candidate of the ruling party suddenly had a comfortable lead.

Unfair election practices can occur at three distinct points: before, during, and after the casting of ballots. Before votes are cast, unfair practices can include preventing certain voters from submitting ballots or allowing some individuals to vote more than once, usually under different names. During the balloting process, certain voting sites in areas known to support one candidate or another can be (intentionally or unintentionally) provided with inadequate staffs or equipment, creating long lines that discourage voters or make it impossible for everyone to vote before closing time. Even more overtly, voting machines can be rigged to under- or overcount votes for certain candidates. Finally, vote tabulations can be misrepresented, either by simply discarding some ballots, miscounting them, or misreporting the final count to election officials.

One vivid example of fraud took place in the 2004 presidential election in the former Soviet country of Ukraine, in which the sitting prime minister was running against a reform candidate. The state-run media heavily favored the prime minister, who was also an ally of the departing president, and opposition activists were harassed and arrested. In western regions of the country that favored the challenger, numerous voters were turned away at the polls, whereas in the central and eastern regions many people registered on the spot under odd circumstances, such as with large groups being brought in by bus to vote. Many unauthorized individuals, including police and local officials, were witnessed being involved with the counting process, and the reported voter turnout was suspiciously high, approaching an extremely unlikely 100 percent in some places. In response, thousands of Ukrainians with orange-colored banners occupied the capital city's main square for days demanding a revote, which the Supreme Court ultimately ordered. In the new vote, the challenger, Victor Yuschenko, won convincingly, leading many to call the entire episode Ukraine's "Orange Revolution." Such a decisive and democratic conclusion to electoral fraud is, sadly, the exception rather than the rule throughout the world.

In the United States, victory in the first two presidential elections of the twenty-first century hinged on the contested election in just a single state: Florida in 2000, and Ohio in 2004. On both occasions, the losing side, the Democrats, alleged a wide range of violations of voting rights. In Florida, it was documented that large numbers of African Americans (known to generally be staunch supporters of the Democrats) were purged from the voting rolls, whereas in Ohio, the registrations of new voters (also mostly believed to be Democrats) were rejected on specious technical grounds. At voting booths, intimidation of voters was reported, such as against Haitian Americans and other non-native English speakers in Florida who might not understand their rights and be easily swayed from voting. Democrats also charged that the voting equipment and services provided to poorer districts were all too much like the schools and other public services provided to those areas: poorly functioning and inadequate. Even more insidious allegations have also been made in Ohio about the use of electronic voting machines that provide no paper trail and thus could be rigged without providing evidence.

Competitive Elections

Even if elections are both free and fair, they cannot be said to fully reflect the will of the people if they are not also competitive—open to all, or nearly all, views held by the general public. Indeed, totalitarian states can, in a technical sense, hold elections that are free and fair but still not democratic if there is but one choice on the ballot. Such elections were quite common in countries of the former Soviet bloc where citizens were required to vote but the only name on the ballot would be that of the designated candidate of the Communist Party. Some dictatorships also stage such "acclamatory elections" and then, in the elaborate fictions that they use to claim legitimacy, point to such election results as evidence of the support of the people.

An only slightly less undemocratic practice in Egypt has led some to accuse long-time President Hosni Mubarak, a twenty-five-year incumbent, of considering himself a modern pharaoh. The Egyptian system allowed only one candidate to be presented to the people after nomination by the legislature—which was itself preserved under the control of a single party. Under international pressure during elections in 2005, Egypt undertook some reforms, but the ruling party still gained unfair advantage through other mechanisms, such as the government's control of mass media and its ability to use government funds to win over supporters. In the theocratic state of Iran, the ruling clerics are empowered to invalidate the candidacy of anyone they deem to be opposed to the values of the revolution they supposedly safeguard, thus ensuring that any candidate they find unacceptable has no chance to compete for office.

As for the competitiveness of elections, at first glance the United States would appear to meet this criterion easily. Beyond a few requirements relating to age, place of residence, and length of citizenship, almost all Americans are eligible to run for almost all public offices (although presidential and vice-presidential candidates must be native-born Americans). At a deeper level, however, it can be argued that U.S. elections are less than fully competitive.

One problem is that of campaigning and media advertising, particularly for higher offices, can be prohibitively expensive, excluding those who cannot raise funds from wealthy donors or self-finance their own campaigns. In some other countries, many of the costs of campaigning are borne to a far greater extent either by political parties or through public resources allocated by the government, such as direct funding or free time on television. In parliamentary systems such as Canada and Britain, campaigns also tend to be much briefer. Unlike the enormously costly eighteen-month marathons that precede U.S. presidential elections, parliamentary elections can unfold within as little as a few weeks because the positions of parties and the qualifications of the leading candidates are generally already well known to the public at large.

Campaigns in the United States, by contrast, are highly candidate centered, with each office-seeker left largely to his or her own means. This has the effect of greatly weakening the power of parties but greatly strengthening the influence of wealthy interests over candidates (and, later, officeholders). The demands of campaign fundraising also help to further reinforce the powerful "incumbency effect" in the United States. Once in office, elected officials can use the resources and influence of their offices to raise funds to all but ensure renomination by their party and then reelection. Strikingly, in most recent elections, 95 percent or more of House members who have sought reelection have won it.

Further, it is extremely unusual for anyone other than a candidate of either the Democratic or the Republican Parties to win an election. Although these two parties aspire to be big tents that include voters and politicians with a wide range of views, some individuals whose views do not fit clearly with either party may find themselves unable to seriously compete for office. (The causes and consequences of the two-party system in the United States are discussed in more detail below and in the next chapter.) In most cases, only the candidate of one party has a realistic chance of winning an election. Increasingly sophisticated software applications are now available to gerrymander electoral districts in the House and in state legislative chambers that cluster together voters in such a way as to all but guarantee either a Republican or Democratic victory.

One factor that makes U.S. elections genuinely more competitive than those of many other countries is the prevalence of primary elections, in which registered members of political parties elect their own nominees for the general election. Having an array of candidates representing differing views (as well as qualifications and personalities) can generate genuine electoral competition within parties. In practice, however, serious primary battles are generally found only when there is an open seat, that is, one that has been vacated by the incumbent. The existence of term limits for many executive offices means that open seats are fairly common in mayoral, gubernatorial, and presidential elections, but much less common in Congress or in those state and city legislatures that do not have term limits. By contrast, the leaders of political parties in many other countries, particularly those with parliamentary systems, simply bestow their party nominations. In this way, such political parties can choose candidates that they feel will support the views of the party leadership—and to punish those office-holders who fail to support the party once they have been elected.

Primary elections can also have the somewhat counterintuitive effect of reducing the competitiveness of moderate candidates in favor of more extreme ones. Consider that in the United States, speaking in rough terms, the most conservative third of voters in the country are likely to be Republicans, the most liberal third are predominantly Democrats, and the moderate middle third are largely independents who have registered to vote but not as members of any party. (Relatively few Americans are registered with minor or third parties.) Usually, only members of a party are eligible to vote in that party's primary elections. The Republican nominees produced by the primary system will thus likely fall somewhere in the middle of the pack of the most conservative third of the country—making them more conservative than about five-sixths of the country. Similarly, the Democratic nominee is likely to be more liberal than all but one-sixth of the country. In reality, candidates nominated in the Democratic and Republican primaries may be even further to the left and the right, respectively, because those voters who turn out to vote in relatively low-profile primary elections are likely to be more ideologically minded than the overall composition of their parties.

When it comes time for all the voters in the general election to choose between the nominees of the Democratic and Republican parties, the moderate candidates who might otherwise appeal to them may have already been excluded from contention. This is not invariably the case because sometimes primary voters endorse the candidate they think is most likely to win the general election rather than the one they may most prefer ideologically. Still, the trend toward excluding moderates is noteworthy. Further, the two-party system also excludes minor party candidates from meaningful contention. In only two elections since World War II (1968 and 1992) has a third-party or independent presidential candidate broken the 10 percent threshold, and no such candidate has gotten more than 20 percent since 1912; the results at other levels of government are scarcely better. Thus, many voters whose views are out of line with the base of the Democratic and Republican parties are likely to find themselves without a clear candidate to support.

Voter Eligibility and Turnout

Another hallmark of democratic elections is a broad right to vote, sometimes called the electoral franchise. The story of U.S. political history is largely one of the expansion of franchise, so that almost all citizens over the age of eighteen are now able to cast ballots. This is a standard commonly applied in democracies around the world, in which restrictions on the right to vote today are rarely abridged by law due to race, ethnicity, or religion. Gender is likewise declining as a reason for exclusion from the right to vote although such barriers persist in a number of mostly Arab states. The voting age is also usually set at around eighteen, although it may vary a few years in either direction.

The United States is rather typical in that voting rights are limited only to citizens. This is to some degree inherent in the logic of rule by the people, which generally defines who are and who are not part of "the people" by whether they hold citizenship. As with most countries, the United States has procedures by which people can become naturalized as citizens and also goes further by providing automatic citizenship to anyone born on American territory or to an American citizen abroad. Some countries define citizenship differently, often based on ethnic descent; for example, generations of ethnic Koreans born in Japan have been denied citizenship—and thus political participation— in that country. Others provide preferential naturalization procedures for some groups, as does Germany for people of ethnic German descent, and as does Israel for those of the Jewish religion.

Even with full voting rights afforded to most adult citizens, Americans do face additional challenges to voting. Some of these are practical, such as the requirement to register to vote and to change one's registration after every move to a new residence. The burden of registration falls entirely on the voter, unlike in some systems in which centralized government records can be used to register voters based on their age and place of residence. Another practical barrier is that in the United States, unlike in many countries, Election Day is not a holiday, making it difficult to get to the polls for some people, such as those with long and inflexible work schedules, heavy childcare responsibilities, or poor transportation in sparsely populated areas.

Further, voting, unlike such civic responsibilities as serving on juries and paying taxes, is not a required activity. In this regard, the United States is typical of the rest of the world, but there are a number of countries, including such democracies as Australia and Brazil, where voting is compulsory. While voting rates do increase when nonvoting is punished by fines or other means, the wisdom of this practice has been questioned. Compulsory voting inevitably means that a large number of poorly informed people will be casting ballots, perhaps subject to misinformation or even bribery. Civil libertarians have also argued that compulsory voting violates freedom of speech by forcing people to register a political opinion.

Another major barrier to voting in the United States is the frequency and complexity of elections in the United States. In this regard, the contrast with Israel is particularly enlightening; as seen in the case study above, elections in Israel are as nearly opposite from elections in the United States as can be imagined between two democracies. Because Israel is a unitary state with a unicameral national parliament, there are no primary elections, no separate elections for executive office, no elections for an upper house of the legislature, no provincial-level elections, and not even any electoral districts (although there are occasional municipal elections). In the United States, voters must cast ballots for a wide array of positions, including president, U.S. senator, U.S. representative, governor, state senator, state assembly member, mayor, city council member, and, sometimes, also state attorneys general, judges, county officers, and a wide variety of other positions. Plus, many states also ask citizens to vote directly on questions of public policy, especially about taxing and spending, through questions placed on the ballot called referenda or initiatives. And citizens may be asked to do this as often as every year or two and then not once but twice, in both party primaries and in general elections.

The complexity and frequency of American elections is often viewed as exacting a heavy toll in terms of "information costs." In order to cast meaningful ballots, voters must not only know when and where to vote but also which positions are open, what these positions do, what the parties stand for, who is running, what their qualifications and records are, and what they have promised to do once in office. Absent any piece of that information, it is hard to cast a meaningful ballot. In a relatively high-literacy country such as the United States, this problem is not as acute as it would be in a developing world context. But there are still considerable numbers of Americans with relatively modest educational backgrounds, and many others for whom English is not their native language.

Finally, characteristics of the U.S. party system and government structure may also help to suppress voter turnout by reducing the perceived relevance of elections among citizens. The effective exclusion of minor parties and the similarities between Democrats and Republicans on many issues means that many voters do not find their own preferences well reflected by the candidates on offer. By contrast, in a multiparty system, various parties will offer widely divergent platforms that are more highly focused on a few key issues: green parties will strongly highlight environmentalism, anti-immigrant parties will focus on border control, rural-based parties will emphasize the needs of farmers, regional parties will agitate for local autonomy, and so on. This panoply of choices provides much more vivid contrasts than the comparatively muddled and centrist platforms typical of two-party systems. Finally, separation of powers and federalism in the United States prevent sudden or sweeping changes in public policy, further reinforcing the idea that "nothing changes" after an election, and leading some to ask themselves why they should even bother to vote.

Taken together, these factors help to explain why the United States has nearly the lowest voter turnout rates found in large and/or populous democracies. In one study of various national elections held in the early 2000s, the U.S. turnout rate of 51.4 percent in the 2000 presidential election was strikingly lower than the highest turnout rates such as 87.4 percent in Italy, 87.0 percent in Iceland, and 82.0 percent in Greece. The U.S. rate was also well below the overall average of 72.1 percent; in fact, only Switzerland had a lower rate of turnout—no coincidence given that Swiss elections are even more complex, and even more frequent, than U.S. elections. It is worth further noting that voter turnout in the United States is at its highest in presidential election years, dropping even further when only lower offices are up for election.

The political significance of the issue of voter turnout has sometimes been questioned, especially in long-established democracies such as the United States. It could well be argued that low voter turnout means that people are relatively content with the political system and that if they were more worried, they would turn out to vote in higher numbers. And, indeed, this was the case in 2004, when voter turnout jumped to 60 percent, its highest level since 1968. Still, low voter turnout can be cause for concern insofar as some groups are far less likely to vote than others, particularly disadvantaged groups such as ethnic and racial minorities and those with low levels of education and income. Although no single cost associated with voting may prove decisive, the cumulative impact of high costs can suppress the turnout of groups who also do not see their own issues and concerns—or their own group members—reflected among the candidates for office and the political parties. When the pool of such alienated citizens grows too large, it can be destabilizing to the political system if they come to feel that they do not have meaningful access to the political system and then turn toward unconventional forms of participation, such as the disruptive protest and political violence discussed in more detail in Chapter 10.

The Winner-Take-All Electoral System

One of the most anomalous features of elections in the United States is also one that many Americans view as virtually synonymous with democracy itself: the idea that there can be one and only one winner in an election. And in the U.S. electoral system, such an outcome is indeed an inevitability. In general elections under a two-party system, one candidate will usually garner an absolute majority of the vote, and that person will take whichever office is at stake. At an instinctual level, Americans tend to view such an outcome at face value. Democracy is equated in the popular mind with majority rule, and the simplest definition of a bare majority is 50 percent of the votes, plus one vote.

When each election can produce one and only one winner, it is hard to argue against such a bare majority rule. If the winner of the election in, for instance, the Fourth Congressional District in Wisconsin is a Republican who receives 60 percent of the vote, it is hard to argue that his or her Democratic challenger should take office instead. But what of the 40 percent who voted against the Republican? There is a good chance that their concerns will be largely overlooked, perhaps for years or decades at a time. This becomes even more problematic when all or part of that 40 percent has some concerns very distinct from the 60 percent majority, such as when they are ethnic, racial, or religious minorities, or are geographically, economically, or ideologically distinctive in some way.

In the U.S. system, called the single-member plurality system, the just outcome is, of course, for the candidate who wins the most votes (the plurality) to take office, for example, to be the single member of the House from a congressional district. But there is nothing in the concept of democracy itself, or even the U.S. Constitution, which demands that the single-member plurality system be used in House races. It is actually only a 1967 law passed by Congress that requires the states with more than one House seat to carve themselves into different congressional districts. Thus, a state whose population gave it ten house seats currently would run ten different elections in ten different districts with ten different winners, each of whom then individually goes to Washington. But constitutionally, the same state could just as easily have one election throughout the state for all ten seats, that is to say it could make itself not a single-member system but a multimember system producing not one but ten election winners.

A number of U.S. states have in the past chosen their House members in this manner, and a variety of cities, counties, and school boards choose all or some of their legislators without the use of districts. (In this case, they are usually called at-large members.) Multimember districting of this type is also used in the majority of democracies in the world today. Indeed, it is for the most part only Britain and former British colonies, such as the United States, Canada, India, and a number of Caribbean island countries, which employ the strict single-member system.

Certainly, the linkage between a particular representative and a distinct, relatively small geographic area does enable legislators to know and serve that small area well and for their constituents to know exactly which single legislator represents them. Indeed, this was the primary rationale for why a single-member plurality system was first introduced for elections to the House of Representatives, the institution of national government that is closest to the people and the only one that was originally directly elected by the people. But this approach can also promote local, parochial interests over broader regional or national interests and can effectively deny minorities a voice in government.

Under a multimember system, there is no longer a requirement that there be a single plurality winner who takes all (i.e., the one and only seat available). While one seat is not divisible, ten seats are, and this makes it possible to move toward a system of proportional representation. Under this system, the focus shifts from individual candidates to parties, which create a party list of as many candidates as there are seats up for election in any given constituency, ranked in the order that the party prefers. Thus, if 60 percent of the voters of a state with ten House seats voted for the Republican Party, then the top six names on the Republican party list would become part of the Wisconsin delegation to the House of Representatives, as would the top four names on the Democratic party list. Rather than being entirely shut out of power, the 40 percent of the state who voted Democratic would be represented by 40 percent of their congressional delegation. (This simple example assumes round numbers, but there are various mathematical formulas available to determine how to convert votes into seats.)

By many counts, proportional representation better reflects the wishes of the electorate than the single-member plurality system. It is perhaps for this reason that some element of proportional representation is used in most democratic countries. As we saw, the system used in Israel is highly representative, with any party that garners over 2 percent of the vote getting a proportional number of seats in the Knesset. Israel is unusual in that all 120 seats of the Knesset are allocated through a nationwide vote. More typically, each province or electoral district of a country will be apportioned a certain number of seats based on its population (as is the case in the United States). This system has led to an exceptional proliferation of political parties in Israel, but multimember proportional representation systems in general reduce the incentive for the maintenance of a two-party system, a theme discussed in greater detail in the next chapter.

In parliamentary systems, in which executive power arises from control of the legislature, it is also possible for executive authority to be distributed across multiple parties, such as by drawing the prime minister from the party with the most seats, but offering other powerful ministerial positions in the cabinet to representatives of smaller parties. The smaller parties can also extract concessions from the larger parties in terms of the government's agenda, further enhancing their role. Under the U.S. system, however, multimember districting would have little or no bearing on the election of executives, such as the president, governors, or mayors, in which one and only one executive office exists. Such elections are by their very nature single-member offices and thus cannot be subject to proportional representation.

Still, by proliferating the number of parties that are able to contest legislative races, proportional representation in the United States could help to expand the number of viable candidates for executive office. Further, there are also other electoral reforms that could enhance the competitiveness of executive elections in the United States. A simple solution would be to have a two-stage election, with the first stage open to all parties and candidates. If no one gets an absolute majority of the votes, then a run-off could be held between the two highest vote getters. Some version of this system is already widely in use for executive elections as diverse as the primary for mayor of New York City, the governorship of Louisiana, and the presidency of France.

A variation on this theme is called instant run-off voting or the single transferable vote. Under this system, voters list two or more candidates in their order of preference. The candidate with the lowest number of votes after the first tabulation is dropped from the election. All of those who selected that candidate as their first choice would have their votes transferred to their second choice candidate for another tabulation. In that way, votes for small parties are not wasted as they are under the current U.S. system, because the voter's preferences are still being accounted for. This process is continued until one candidate has an absolute majority of votes.

This system would directly address the criticism that voting for minor party candidates is pointless since they almost certainly will not win, and that such voting may even indirectly contribute to the election of the voter's least favorite candidate. A striking example comes from the year 2000, when many more left-wing voters might have cast their vote for Green Party candidate Ralph Nader in an instant run-off election, secure in the knowledge that if Nader were eliminated their second choice, presumably Al Gore, would then receive their vote. Under current rules, those left-leaning citizens who voted for Nader rather than Gore prevented Gore from winning enough votes in the Electoral College to defeat Nader's ideological opposite, George W. Bush.

Peculiarities of the U.S. Presidential Elections

No discussion of U.S. voting and elections would be complete without an examination of one of the most unusual yet influential of all electoral features: the institution of the Electoral College. Indeed, it is hard to overstate the peculiarities of this method of selecting the president, a method which is neither entirely direct nor entirely indirect. Fearful of allowing the people to directly choose an executive, the founders created instead a nebulously defined intermediate institution of electors. Mindful of states' rights, they gave the power to determine how electors are chosen to the legislature in each state. And eager to capitalize on their hard-won compromise balancing the interests of large and small states, slave and free states in Congress, they simply imported that same formula into the method for selecting presidents, with each state having the same number of electors as it has members of the House and the Senate combined.

As democracy became more entrenched, every state in the union decided that their electors would automatically be allocated on the basis of the popular vote in that state. But in order to maximize their impact on the election, all except two states decided to employ a system in which whoever receives the most votes in that state gets all of that state's electoral votes. This has long had the effect of giving the victors in presidential elections a far larger share of the electoral vote than the popular vote, but for over a century the winner in the popular vote still was always the winner in the electoral vote.

That changed, of course, in the year 2000 when Al Gore won the popular vote by more than half a million votes but received four fewer electoral votes than George W. Bush as a result of the contested election in Florida. This anomalous outcome brought closer scrutiny to the Electoral College, and some of its other oddities. It was noted, for instance, that voters today still do not actually cast their ballot for a particular candidate for president, but rather for electors who have pledged to cast an electoral vote in support of a particular candidate. Because the electors are chosen by the political parties, they are considered to be reliable when it comes time to cast their electoral vote the way they pledged, but it is not clear how effectively electors can really be bound to do so; indeed, in 2000 one Democratic elector cast a blank ballot (rather than one for Gore) in protest of the Florida outcome.

And there are still other peculiarities. It is entirely possible that, had the outcome of a recount gone to Gore, the Republican-controlled Florida state legislature could have used their constitutional authority to appoint a slate of electors of their choosing regardless of the popular vote outcome. And the closeness of the election also brought about reminders that if no candidate received an absolute majority of 270 of the 538 electoral votes, then it would be up to the House of Representatives to choose the president. Not only would this be something of a violation of the general principle of separation of powers, but each state's entire House delegation would collectively cast just one vote, drastically inflating the influence of low-population states.

Certainly, no one would design the Electoral College today, yet it persists. As we have seen, it is enormously difficult to amend the Constitution, particularly around issues that might weaken the position of the low-population states. Defenders of the system have argued that the Electoral College system has some benefits, such as forcing a presidential candidate to amass support throughout many areas of the country. Others have noted that the winner-take-all system focuses campaign time and energy disproportionately on higher-population so-called "swing states" such as Ohio and Florida, in which a relatively large pot of electoral votes could potentially be won by either candidate. But what is definitely clear is that the Electoral College is one of the most anomalous of all institutions of American democracy.

Even without the Electoral College, U.S. presidential elections would still be unusually long, arduous, and unpredictable. As early as two years before the election, contenders begin to emerge from one or both of the major political parties, especially when no sitting president will be running for reelection. These presidential aspirants then embark on a more than year-long marathon of policy speeches, campaign stops, media appearances, and fundraising efforts, all under the searing scrutiny of the national press. They must also undertake relentless fundraising efforts to garner the tens of millions of dollars needed to mount a viable national campaign. Soon, the rise and fall of poll numbers, fundraising, endorsements, and many other factors contribute to a horse-race mentality, with some candidates seen to be gaining ground and others falling behind. And all of this comes before they ever get to the first of the party primary elections (or, in some states, caucuses) used to allocate each state party's electoral support to specific candidates.

Because different states hold their primaries on different days over the course of several months, the horse-race mentality intensifies until one candidate captures enough support to be assured of that party's nomination. (This occurs more quickly on the Republican than Democratic side because the Democrats use a proportional representation system in their presidential primary.) The party nomination will be bestowed at a coronation-like national party convention during the summer before the election. At this point, the nominees must simultaneously try to patch up relations with the rivals they had fought throughout the primaries, shore up the support of the base voters within their party, and also begin reaching out to the centrist voters needed to win in November. Then the campaign is resumed with a focus on the other major party's candidate in the general election, in which the peculiar institution of the Electoral College takes center stage.

By contrast, the elections in parliamentary democracies are far quicker and more predictable and are usually much less about personalities than about support for the specific public policies of different parties. Because parliamentary elections do not occur on a clearly fixed schedule and because they have no primary election phase, the entire process can be collapsed into just a few weeks; in Britain, for instance, they must by law occur within seventeen working days after the prime minister calls for elections. Such a truncated timetable is possible because potential prime ministers, having worked their way to the leadership of a major party, are usually already well known, long-established politicians on the national stage. For better or worse, parliamentary systems rarely produce a prime minister who is an outsider to the existing political elite.

On balance, the U.S. system does allow for a great deal of competition, a long timetable during which the people can scrutinize the candidates, and a rough-and-tumble debate over opposing values and views. It can also sometimes allow talented newcomers a window of opportunity and can bring fresh perspectives to office. On the other hand, the U.S. system often results in winners, notably state governors, with no prior national-level experience and with whom most Americans had little familiarity before the election process. Due to their length and complexity, U.S. presidential elections can have many twists and turns and seem to hinge on trivial incidents and personal foibles that have little to do with the candidates' fitness for office, political skills, or views of public policy. Few would argue that the arduous and expensive American way of electing its chief executives consistently produces the best possible results.

Conclusion

Elections are essential to democracy, but electoral systems also shape the form that democracy will take in any particular country. The winner-take-all system used in the United States is a rarity, with most countries of the world using some form of proportional representation (PR) so that elections more closely reflect the wishes of voters. The use of PR can have significant implications for democratic practice, such as increasing voter turnout and providing a broad array of voices in government. One of its major impacts is the promotion of multiparty rather than two-party political systems, a theme discussed in greater detail in the next chapter.

Further Reading

* *Electoral Engineering: Voting Rules and Political Behavior.* Pippa Norris. Cambridge University Press, New York: 2004.
* *Elections as an Instrument of Democracy: Majoritarian and Proportional Visions.* G. Bingham Powell, Jr. Yale University Press, New Haven CT: 2000.
* *Voter Turnout and the Dynamics of Electoral Competition in Established Democracies since 1945.* Mark N. Franklin. Cambridge University Press, New York: 2004.

Web-Based Exploration Exercise

Examine the voting system of any three other countries, at least one of which uses a proportional representation system in its elections. Identify and discuss any one similarity and one difference with the U.S. system of elections. A useful Website for information about elections worldwide can be found at <www.psr.keele.ac.uk/election.htm>.

Question for Debate and Discussion

Low voter turnout is an unusual and even somewhat embarrassing feature of politics in the United States, which has often held itself to be a model of democratic practice. To what extent and in what ways is lower voter turnout problematic? Are there features of other political systems that could usefully be adapted to the U.S. system in order to increase voter turnout? Would it be worthwhile to carry out such changes?

9

POLITICAL PARTIES AND
INTEREST GROUPS

Political parties and interest groups are two forms of political participation that are central to American democracy, yet are entirely unmentioned in the Constitution. Indeed, James Madison, in *Federalist 10,* famously warned against the "mischief of faction" in which groups pursuing their own goals undermine the collective good. Yet it would be hard to imagine how the U.S. political system would function in the absence of political parties to provide broad alternatives to the electorate and interest groups to aggregate and articulate the political agendas of a profusion of smaller, more specialized subgroupings.

A particularly unusual feature in the United States is that since 1800 there have been two and only two major parties at any one time—and that since 1860, these have been the same two parties: the Democrats and the Republicans. Although their geographical bases and their ideological positions have shifted over time, these same two major parties have provided stable, predictable choices for the American electorate and organizing structures within American government. No president since the unanimously elected George Washington has hailed from a minor party, nor has either house of Congress had more than a smattering of nonmajor party members. As of this writing, 533 of 535 seats in Congress, all 50 state governorships, and all but a handful of seats in the nation's 99 state legislative chambers are held by either Democrats or Republicans.

The monopolization of power in the United States by just two parties is such a fact of political life that many Americans might be surprised to learn that such a long-term two-party system is a true anomaly in the world. Indeed, far more common are countries in which two centrist parties predominate—one somewhat left of center and one somewhat right of center—but a variety of other smaller parties regularly affect the outcome of elections and win some offices. Some of these are so-called two-party-plus systems, while others are true multiparty systems of four or more parties. The number of parties can have a major effect on the politics of a country in terms both of how voters are represented by their elected officials and how political views are translated into public policy. In part because there are just two political parties in the United States, the interest group sector is unusually robust, offering an additional and more varied layer of representation by a large number of very active organizations and associations.

A Hypothetical Case Study:
Electoral Systems and the Number of Parties

As discussed in the last chapter, the number of parties in a political system that can actually contend for power is largely determined by characteristics of the electoral system. The single-member plurality electoral system used in the United States thus is a major reason for the two-party system in the United States. Recall that under this system each election can result in one, and only one, winner—namely, whichever candidate gains more votes than any other candidate. The French political scientist Maurice Duverger has argued that most modern democracies have broad electorates that are divided by class, region, religion, ethnicity, and a number of other factors. Such countries, states Duverger's Law, will naturally gravitate toward creating a multiparty system unless, as in the United States, the country's electoral system "punishes" the proliferation of parties.

To understand the connection between electoral systems and the number of parties, it may be helpful to consider a hypothetical case study focusing on two dimensions of political disagreement that can be found in most countries: between conservatism and liberalism over economic issues and over social issues. Suppose that 40 percent of the country has economic conservatism as their major policy concern. They might form an Economic Conservative (EC) Party favoring low taxes, probusiness policies, and limited government regulation of the economy. Another 30 percent of the country might be economic liberals, whose EL Party supports social welfare programs that redistribute income, policies that favor labor unions, and heavy government involvement in economic issues. Suppose that the remainder of the electorate is more focused on social than economic issues, with 20 percent being social liberals and the remaining 10 percent being social conservatives. The resulting SL Party and SC Party likely would be in conflict over such social issues as abortion, prayer in schools, and gay rights.

Now imagine an election to a national legislature in which each of the four parties fielded its own candidates and garnered a percentage of the vote exactly equal to its support among voters, but under two different electoral systems: single-member plurality and multimember proportional representation. In the single-member plurality system, the EC Party, with its 40 percent total, has a plurality of the votes and wins the one seat being contested in that particular election. The 60 percent of the population who voted *against* the EC Party have no representation. In effect, the smaller parties have been punished by the single-member plurality system. So what would happen next?

Upset at their exclusion from power and seeking a new electoral strategy, the second-place finisher, the EL Party, might very well seek an alliance with another party. Their most likely alliance would be with the SL Party that shares some of their basic ideology of equality and fairness even if not all of their specific policy preferences. The merger of the 30 percent of voters who are economic liberals and 20 percent of voters who are social liberals into a new Unified Liberal Party would bring their percentage of the vote to about 50 percent, meaning that they would be ensured the most votes in the next election. With a bit of luck and a good campaign, they might even be able to win enough voters from other parties to push themselves just up above the 50 percent mark and thus be assured of victory. Naturally, the economic conservatives would note this development and begin to court the social conservatives, with whom they share a concern about individual responsibility and social order. Together, they will be able to create a new Unified Conservative Party to meet the threat of the Unified Liberal Party.

By the next election, then, we will have seen Duverger's Law in action, and the country will have created a two-party system, with each party fighting to win just a small advantage over the other by winning over undecided, mostly centrist voters. The new, larger parties will have to orient themselves toward a broader set of concerns and accept greater ideological variation among their members. Rather than having the sharper focus of the smaller parties, the new larger parties will likely be big tents that can accommodate a majority of the country's electorate. (By now, some readers may have noted that this case study is not *entirely* hypothetical; a large coalition of economic and social conservatives is not a bad way to describe the U.S. Republican Party, while the U.S. Democratic Party might well be considered a broad umbrella organization of economic and social liberals.)

The results of the exact same election would play out very differently under a system of proportional representation with multimember districts. Under this system, there would likely be multiple legislative seats up for election, say ten for the sake of simplicity and round numbers. Under this system, the EC Party would take four seats (40 percent); the EL Party three seats (30 percent); the SL Party two seats (20 percent); and the SC Party one seat (10 percent). Thus, none of the principal parties would have been denied representation; they would each be sending at least one member to the legislature where they could make speeches, introduce legislation, and engage in debates that clearly represent the views of their voters. If this were a parliamentary system, they might even have the opportunity to join in a coalition government, perhaps holding a cabinet position in a ministry that is very important to their voters. While parties might make a strategic decision to join a coalition so as to benefit their members, there would be little incentive to lose their individual organizational and ideological identities by merging into two large parties. Thus, a multiparty system would become established, perhaps even adding additional parties over time.

Single-Party Systems

Before we consider the merits of a two-party versus a multiparty system, it is worth noting that a number of nondemocratic countries have only a single functioning party, with all other parties either formally outlawed or prevented from gaining power through various legal and extralegal means. The party in such situations may play a leading role in the society, usually based on some elaborate religious, nationalistic, or other ideological justification. Formal membership in the party may be extended to the most prominent and powerful people in the country, forming a ruling stratum that dominates the entire country. Such has often been the case in Communist countries, but similar dynamics can be found in a number of other countries, such as the Baathist Party in Syria and, formerly, in Iraq. Such arrangements were discussed in the section on nondemocratic executives in Chapter 5, and will not be reviewed here. Suffice it to say that in these cases the word *party* has a rather different meaning than that used in democratic countries, closer to that of a regime with a monopoly on power than of a group that contends for power via the ballot box.

Two-Party-Plus Systems

As the hypothetical case study suggests, the roots of the American two-party system are largely a function of the electoral system used in the United States, but this is not the sole explanation. The single-member plurality system has indeed led to rigid two-party structures in a number of other former British colonies, such as the relatively small island nations of Jamaica, Barbados, the Bahamas, and Malta. However, larger and more diverse countries that make use of the single-member plurality system do not exclude minor party participation nearly as much as in the United States. Some of these countries, notably Britain and Canada, have been termed two-party-plus systems. In these countries, only the two major parties in each country have any real hope of forming a parliamentary majority, but at least one other small party continues to win seats in parliament, to meaningfully influence political debate, and sometimes even hold the balance of power in the parliament.

Control of parliament in Canada, for instance, has for generations alternated between a center-left party, the Liberals, and a center-right party, the Conservatives (under various party names). However, there are two other parties that regularly win seats in the House of Commons. One, the socialist New Democratic Party (NDP), has often won between 15 and 20 percent of the national vote and some real influence in parliament. Since 1990, the country has also had a regionally based party representing French speakers at the national level, with a parallel party operating within the province of Quebec. In Britain, control of parliament alternates between the Tories, the conservative party, and the Labour Party, traditionally based upon the support of labor unions. Before the rise of Labour after World War II, the Liberal Party had been one of the two major parties, but rather than vanish, it has remained a significant third force in British politics, emphasizing individual liberty and holding a considerable number of seats in local government. Meanwhile, a small number of regional parties also regularly elect candidates from Scotland, Wales, and Northern Ireland.

Since both Britain and Canada use the single-member plurality system, it seems clear that the electoral system cannot be the sole explanation of the preponderance of the two major parties in the United States. In understanding why minor parties are so marginalized in U.S. politics, at least three additional factors should be considered. The first is that most developed countries have a greater range of ideological differences than the United States. The British Labour Party and the Canadian NDP have both traditionally been socialist parties, meeting the need for the party system in those countries to stretch from laissez-faire market capitalism all the way to redistributive socialism—too far a reach for just two parties. The historical failure of socialism in the United States (for reasons discussed in Chapters 10 and 11) has resulted in a much shorter spectrum of views that could be considered mainstream.

Secondly, the Scots, Welsh, and Northern Irish consider themselves separate nations from the majority English in Britain, and the Quebecois view themselves as a distinct society within Canada, providing added impetus for the maintenance of ethnically based minor parties. The United States, however, is indisputably one nation. From time to time, regional candidates in the United States have attempted to form separate parties, as when Southern Democrats ran for president in 1948 and 1968 as the candidates of break-away parties focused on states' rights, winning thirty-nine and forty-six electoral votes, respectively. But these have been short-lived, and ultimately ineffective, efforts. Further, the Democratic and Republican Parties in the United States are quite decentralized when compared with parties in other countries. Thus, Republicans in New England or Democrats in the Deep South, who may be at odds with the leadership of their national parties, have a great deal of latitude and flexibility in how they conduct their affairs. This further diminishes the temptation that regional parties might have to break away from the national party that might be found in more rigidly centralized party systems.

Finally, minor parties in a parliamentary system have some hope of entering into a coalition to share in executive power, but in the United States the president is elected separately and is an office held by only a single individual. Further, the rules of the Electoral College make it even more difficult for a minor party to be a contender because most states allocate their electoral votes such that the winner of the plurality takes all of that state's electoral votes. Thus, minor party candidate H. Ross Perot won 19 percent of the popular vote for president in 1992 and 8 percent in 1996 but received zero electoral votes both times because he never won an entire state. With control of the executive firmly out of reach, it is especially difficult for any third party in the United States to gather much steam on a national basis, further deterring the emergence of a two-party-plus system in the United States. Similar factors make it difficult for third parties to establish a foothold even at the state level, from which they might grow into national contenders from power, although independent candidates have occasionally been successful in winning governorships.

Multiparty Systems

In contrast to two-party and two-party-plus systems are those in which four, five, six—or even more than a dozen—parties regularly contend for power. At the lower end of this spectrum are countries that have a relatively high threshold for entry into parliament, thus minimizing the role of more extreme parties. In Germany, for instance, a party must receive 5 percent of the national vote to be allocated any seats in the Bundestag under proportional representation rules. This has had the effect of diminishing the electoral appeal of extreme parties, most notably the far-right Republikaner Party and the former Communist Party of East Germany, both of which have been excluded from the Bundestag. Further, Germany uses a mixed electoral system in which each voter casts two votes, one for a seat to be decided under the single-member plurality system and a second for seats allocated on the basis of proportional representation using party lists. The use of the single-member plurality system to choose half of the Bundestag helps to reduce the number of parties, just as it does in Britain and Canada. Despite these factors, Germany still has four major parties: two large parties, the center-right Christian Democrats and the center-left Social Democrats, and two smaller parties, the progressive Green Party and the conservative Free Democratic Party. This has led to a great deal of stability in German politics, with control alternating between the Christian Democrats and the Social Democrats, often in coalition with a smaller party.

Once the threshold for entry into parliament is lowered even further, the number of parties proliferates. As seen in the last chapter, Israel has only a 2 percent threshold and a pure proportional representation system. In 2006, twelve parties won seats in the Knesset, showing far more diversity and variation than found in most other countries. Three of the largest parties represented more or less the classic span of left-wing, centrist, and right-wing parties (Labour, Kadima, and Likud), but others included parties drawing support specifically from Israeli Arabs, Russian Jewish emigres, and Jews of Sephardic, or Mediterranean, ancestry. Ideologically, the parties ranged from the unabashedly Communist to the stridently nationalistic. Further instability is added to the Israeli party system by the frequent appearance of new, and disappearance of old, parties. In fact, the party that won the most votes, Kadima, was contesting its first election in 2006.

The same threshold of 2 percent and pure proportional representation also prevails in Italy, with even more fragmented results in that country's 2006 elections. Nine parties on the left won more than 2 percent of the vote, including two separate Communist parties, as did five parties on the right, including one party with fascist roots and another sympathetic to separatist impulses in the wealthy north of Italy. The electoral situation in Italy was not quite as chaotic as it may seem, however, because many of the parties had formed various electoral alliances prior to the vote, so that protracted postelection coalition negotiations were not needed. Still, the end result was a razor-thin margin for the left, which was bitterly contested for a time, and the government fell due to a vote of no confidence just nine months later. As discussed in Chapter 4, the long history of unstable party coalitions in Italy has seriously hampered the ability of the government to tackle violence, corruption, and inequality in that country.

In the case of both Israel and Italy, the fragmentation of the party system both reflects and reinforces preexisting ideological, socioeconomic, religious, regional, and other tensions in those countries. However, multiparty systems do not necessarily lead to greater discord. The Nordic nations, for instance, have multiparty systems but also have political cultures in which broad coalition governments are created with little rancor, or else in which minority governments can be allowed by the opposition to rule without being brought down by early votes of no confidence. Clearly, the relative ethnic homogeneity and socioeconomic equality of the citizenry in such countries as Norway, Sweden, and Denmark help to promote a sense of national cooperation.

Somewhat counterintuitively, however, multiparty systems can also be used to bridge differences within highly diverse countries. Two of the most ethnically divided long-term democracies in Europe are Belgium, with two major linguistic communities, and Switzerland, with three. Yet both of these countries also created formal and informal power-sharing agreements across political parties that foster consensus over conflict. In all of these examples, it is probably the case that consensus building has been greatly aided by economic prosperity and social tranquility, and also by a high degree of decentralized power through robust federalism. Switzerland, which has a unique seven-member executive, has gone so far as to establish the so-called "Magic Formula" in which a set number of the seven slots go to representatives of particular parties and language groups. In Belgium, linguistic communities can block legislation that might affect their fundamental interests.

Sadly for the most divided and unstable countries of the world, it seems that such consensus arrangements, sometimes called "consociational democracies," must evolve naturally within a country and cannot be imposed from outside. Attempts to establish a delicate consociational political balance among the Christians, Sunni Muslims, and Shiite Muslims of Lebanon broke down in 1975 into a bloody fifteen-year civil war. A consociational solution would have been ideal in the case of Bosnia, as discussed in Chapter 2, but deep-seated animosities have at least thus far prevented any such creative solutions there. The prospects for a consociational solution seem even more remote for Iraq, where attempts to promote power sharing among the Sunni Arab, Shiite Arab, and Kurdish populations descended into civil war in 2006.

The U.S. Two-Party System in Comparative Perspective

What does it mean for the U.S. political system that the same two political parties have vied for power for over two thirds of the country's history? Certainly, one major impact has been a tremendous degree of stability when compared with the many countries where new parties are created, splinter, merge, or vanish on a regular basis. Although their geographical bases and their ideological positions have shifted over time, the same two major parties have for nearly 150 years provided stable, predictable choices for the American electorate and organizing structures within American government.

The downside of stability, of course, can be inflexibility, inertia, and even stagnation. With the same two parties all but assured of dominance, it can be hard for new voices and new ideas to enter the U.S. political system. In particular, minor parties in the United States struggle to make an impression of any kind. Throughout continental Europe, for instance, environmentalism-oriented Green Parties have flourished, but the U.S. Green Party has struggled to elect even a few state legislators. Not entirely coincidentally, the two major parties have been promising for generations to advance research on clean alternative fuel sources with little real progress, nor has the major challenge of global warming been seriously addressed.

Similarly, the Reform Party that emerged with the presidential candidacy of H. Ross Perot in 1992 and 1996 rose meteorically and fell just as quickly, garnering less than 1 percent of the vote in 2000 and splintering thereafter. Although the Reform Party was unable to mount a challenge to the two-party system, it did influence the national agenda. After Perot won 19 percent of the popular vote in 1992, both the Democrats and Republicans quickly repositioned themselves to capture the Reform Party's signature issue, which was concern about the federal deficit. The once seemingly unconquerable issue of the budget deficit was suddenly resolved in the mid-1990s, a time when the country was awash in surpluses. There were several factors contributing to this shift, such as high tax revenues from a robust economy, but the electoral challenge posed by the Reform Party was certainly a contributing factor. Thus the experience of the Reform Party is typical in that minor parties are more likely to alter the positions of the major parties rather than to achieve any direct impact or win offices themselves. Critics charge, however, that once the groundswell of support for a particular minor party has been co-opted, its fragile institutions undermined, and its threat dissipated, politics as usual is restored; consider the return of budget deficits after 2001.

The U.S. two-party system has also been faulted for denying voters the opportunity to support a party that clearly reflects their own views. The larger the number of parties in a country, the narrower the set of issues on which each party tends to focus. To return to the hypothetical case study above, if a country had four parties based on economic conservatism, social conservatism, economic liberalism, and social liberalism, each of those parties would be fairly tightly focused on a core set of issues and concerns. Both during elections and in government, the economic conservative party would emphasize policies that benefit business and promote economic growth. The social conservative party would focus on topics that they see as contributing to a decline in social order and traditional values. The economic liberal party would stress the need to protect labor unions and redistribute income. And the social liberal party would concentrate on minority rights and diversity concerns. Although any of these parties might have to compromise to some degree if they entered a coalition to create a parliamentary majority, the individual parties would not lose their separate organizational structures nor their basic priorities. When the number of parties proliferates further, as in Israel and Italy, then each party can become even more specialized, such as by focusing on the concerns of specific ethnic groups, religious beliefs, or regions.

However, when a country has only two parties, both must be "big tents" large enough to encompass the views and garner the support of at least 50 percent of the electorate. Such parties can become vague and unfocused in their platforms, trying to appease an overly broad array of conflicting views. Thus voters are less likely to see their own views clearly articulated by either of the parties and must tolerate the presence within their party of views with which they may strongly disagree.

Exactly such a muddled situation emerged in 2006 on the issue of immigration in the United States. The economic conservative wing of the Republican Party sought to maintain a steady supply of inexpensive labor, proposing various guest worker programs. Social conservatives within the Republican Party, in contrast, tended to see illegal aliens as lawbreakers who should be punished. A parallel debate also emerged in the Democratic Party, with economic liberals, who are often allied with labor unions, concerned that low-cost labor may undermine the wages of American workers. Meanwhile social liberals in the Democratic Party tended to view undocumented immigrants as a vulnerable minority in need of social services and protection from exploitation. United States voters thus could not look to a single party that clearly reflected their own views on the issue of immigration, whereas in a multiparty system they might be offered clear policy alternatives by several parties. The result was largely infighting, political paralysis, and an incoherent policy that fails to monitor immigrants, defend the borders, maximize economic benefits, or protect human rights.

The two-party system in the United States is also related to the striking narrowness and rightward tilt of the American ideological spectrum (a theme which is discussed from a historical perspective in Chapters 10 and 11). Critics from both the right and the left have argued that the Democratic and Republican parties are barely distinguishable from one another. Ralph Nader, a leftist presidential candidate in 2000, took to calling his opponents "Republicrats," while George Wallace, an archconservative presidential candidate in 1968, famously declared that there "isn't a dime's worth of difference between the parties." While these are overstatements, they do underline the reality that the Democrats and the Republicans are clearly distinguishable on only a relative handful of issues, such as abortion, taxation, and some elements of foreign policy. Both parties are in basic agreement on the majority of public policy issues. Such similarity between the two major parties is in marked contrast to the broader political spectrum found in multiparty democracies. As noted above, the parties represented in the Italian parliament stretch from the far left, essentially old-style Communism, to the far right, with some roots in Mussolini-era fascism. Further, the leaders of such parties in Western Europe are often household names, not the obscure, marginalized figures of their ideological counterparts in the United States.

In addition to being relatively similar to one another on many issues, both the Democratic and Republican parties are more conservative than most parties in the developed world. A useful comparison can be made between the presidential elections held in 2002 in France and in 2000 in the United States. In the first of two rounds of presidential voting in France, President Jacques Chirac ran for reelection as the candidate of the center-right, while Prime Minister Lionel Jospin represented the center-left. The French far left fragmented among a variety of Communist and other minor party candidates, while the far right mostly coalesced around Jean-Marie Le Pen, the longtime leader of the xenophobic National Front.

In 2000 in the United States, the center-right candidate was then-Texas Governor George W. Bush, the center-left candidate was Vice President Al Gore, the far-left candidate was Ralph Nader of the Green Party, and the far-right candidate was political pundit Pat Buchanan. However, terms such as center, left, and right are all relative and can vary from country to country. Indeed, had Gore been running in the French presidential election, his policies regarding such issues as the rate of taxation, regulation of the economy, and government spending on social services would have placed him somewhat to the *right* of the French center-right candidate Chirac. Bush's political views would have situated him about midway between Chirac and Le Pen, while many of Buchanan's positions would put him quite near LePen. Because LePen and another rightist candidate took about 20 percent of the vote, this means that 80 percent of French voters cast a ballot for Chirac and other presidential candidates who were further to the *left* than Al Gore. Only Nader, who won under 3 percent of the U.S. popular vote, held political views similar to those of the large majority of the French. This leftward tilt of the political systems found in France is largely emblematic of that found throughout Western Europe.

A final characteristic of the U.S. party system that bears reiteration here is their relative weakness when compared with parties in countries with parliamentary democracies. As discussed in the previous chapter, party leaders in parliamentary democracies typically have several major sources of strength lacking in the United States: they control nominations during elections as well as upward career mobility from backbenchers to ministerial positions. The decentralization of the party system in the United States is also a factor. In many countries, particularly unitary states, there is likely to be one powerful national organization for each party, with local or provincial branches simply carrying out the wishes of the national party. In the United States, however, there are separate party organizations in every state that are quasi-independent and only partly subject to the demands of the national party organization.

The U.S. parties also have limited sway over the rank-and-file members of the party. In this sense, the Republicans and Democrats are good examples of so-called cadre parties in that most political activity is undertaken by a relatively small core of leaders and activists. In the United States, the party identification of voters can be quite a significant factor in the way that they view political issues and how they vote, but some voters still regularly cross lines to support candidates of the opposite party. Such cadre parties are in contrast to so-called mass membership parties, most notably Labor Parties, in which membership in a labor union and in the party is simultaneous. In such mass membership parties, rank-and-file members may be much more influential in the setting of party policy positions than in cadre parties. But, in turn, these parties can make much more compelling ideological and psychological claims on the loyalties of their members.

Despite these weaknesses, the two major U.S. parties do still have an exceptional measure of clout in that they have long been the only electorally viable parties, and on some levels collude to maintain their long-term claims to power. For instance, the two parties have used their longstanding monopoly on power to make it difficult for third parties to emerge, such as by creating demanding rules for access to the ballot and high thresholds for public financing and participation in campaign debates. In this regard, the Democrats and Republicans fare better than many of their counterparts in other separation-of-powers systems. Political parties are particularly weak in most of Latin America, where the separation-of-powers system is combined with the use of proportional representation in legislative elections. Thus, not only do Latin American parties lack the tools to impose party discipline that are found in parliamentary countries, but they also experience the fragmentation into multiple parties that comes from the use of proportional representation. This weakness of the party system is another contributing factor in the political instability commonly found in Central and South America.

Interest Groups

The relative weakness of political parties may, in part, explain the unusually large role played by interest groups in U.S. politics. Although the United States has only two large major parties, the political system also includes a profusion of interest groups of nearly every conceivable variety and size. While the ideological spectrum is exceptionally narrow in the electoral realm, U.S. interest groups stretch from the far right to the far left. And, whereas parties are comparatively weak, interest groups are unusually strong in their cumulative impact on U.S. politics.

Because the purpose of interest groups is to seek benefits from government, interest group activity in the United States parallels the fragmentation of the U.S. governmental structure. Interest groups operate at the local, state, and national level, some mainly at one level, others at multiple levels. They may also target legislators, executives, and bureaucrats at all levels; a considerable number also engage in litigation strategies that involve various levels of courts. Further, because of the relative autonomy of American politicians from the control of political parties, interest groups must form connections directly with elected officials and their staffs rather than simply with party leaders. Finally, at least since the time of the great French observer Alexis de Tocqueville, it has been noted that Americans have an exceptional propensity toward joining voluntary associations of all sorts. All of these influences—plus the sheer size and diversity of the United States—have led to the creation of an unusually large and decentralized universe of interest groups in the United States. Such a system is in marked contrast to unitary states with parliamentary systems in which the geographic and institutional concentration of power would lead most interest group activity to be focused on the executive branch of government and in the national capital.

Although many U.S. interest groups naturally ally themselves with one party or the other, they need not work through party structures. Public interest groups concerned about, say, the environment or gun rights, would find little utility in pressuring the national organizations of the Democratic or Republican Parties, as these have very limited direct influence on officeholders. Instead, interest groups must approach individual legislators or executives directly. To be effective in the United States, interest groups must have the funding, expertise, and support to offer a variety of resources to politicians, including expert advice during the legislative process, endorsements at election time, and get-out-the-vote activities of various types.

The clearest, and also perhaps most pernicious, linkage between interest groups and officeholders comes in the form of campaign donations to politicians who rely mostly on their own fundraising abilities to fund expensive and near-continuous reelection activities. Interest groups that represent wealthy sectors in any country have clear-cut material advantages over those representing poorer and disadvantaged sectors. But in the United States, the skew is even more pronounced than in countries with parliamentary systems in which there are fewer offices open for election, campaigns are shorter, individual candidates have fewer fundraising pressures, and the public sector often provides funding, free television time, and other resources during campaigns. Campaign financing is so important that it has been argued that some powerful interest groups in the United States are able to virtually dictate public policy in the areas of concern to them.

They do so, it is argued, by providing crucial financial and other support, such as endorsements, to members of Congress who sit on key committees, enabling them to write legislation and pressure the federal bureaucracy on the interest groups' behalf. The result is that some powerful interest groups can come to dominate the government decision making in specific small areas, forming what have been termed subgovernments or iron triangles. Such arrangements can be found in governments around the world, but they particularly flourish in a political system with weak parties, wide dispersal of legislative and executive authority, and decentralized bureaucracies.

Despite these informal flows of influence, interest groups in the United States rarely have any sort of official status or sanction awarded by the government. By contrast, a number of other countries employ a system sometimes called "corporatism" in which a small number of groups representing major social sectors play a more or less official role in government decision making. (This traditional use of the term *corporatism* is only partly related to the more recent popular use of the term to criticize the excessive influence of wealthy business corporations.) In Sweden, a single federation of labor is officially recognized by the state as the organization with which it negotiates wage levels. In Japan, a federation of economic organizations has played a major role in negotiating export policies. And in France, a national farmers' federation has worked with the government to modernize French agriculture. In each of these cases, the partnership between the state and a single representative of powerful interests has promoted social harmony, although sometimes at the risk of subsequent inflexibility in policy formulation.

When powerful economic interests have such a direct role in the work of government, it can be hard for the state to later extract concessions from them when economic circumstances change. This is less of a problem in authoritarian countries, such as China, where corporatist arrangements are sometimes created in order to provide expertise to state policymakers and then to help with carrying out the decisions of those policymakers with little or no questioning. By contrast, in the United States, interest groups function in a much more competitive environment, each struggling to have its influence felt. There is, for instance, no single labor association or single association of business interests that is formally empowered to speak on behalf of that entire sector of the economy or to participate in the work of government.

Another notable pattern in the United States is that labor unions are simply one type of interest group among many. Union membership in the United States has been declining for many years, but even at its height, unions never played the central role in American politics that they have played elsewhere, especially in Western Europe where class divisions have always been more pronounced. In some of those countries, labor unions formed the nucleus of political parties that have, in many cases, emerged as a major force in the politics of their countries. The British Labour party was a particularly good example of that in the 1960s and 1970s, when that country's Trade Union Congress essentially controlled the party that, in turn, often controlled government. In some other countries, the linkages were not quite that direct, but governments sometimes provide official recognition of labor federations, which are given a role in policy formulation. By comparison, U.S. labor unions have generally been strong supporters of the Democratic Party but have formed just one part of that party's large electoral base.

Just as neither labor nor interest groups hold official status in the United States, neither do any religious groups or denominations enjoy the status of being the official religion of the state. Perhaps the classic example of an established church is in Britain, where the head of state, the king or queen, is also the head of the Church of England and the nation's Anglican bishops officially hold seats in the House of Lords as "lords spiritual." The Catholic Church has also held official status as the church of the state in a number of countries, such as Spain and Ireland. The secularization of Western Europe has rendered these relationships largely obsolete, although the Catholic Church and various Orthodox Christian churches still exert considerable sway in parts of Eastern Europe. The special status given to Islam in many Muslim countries is today a more relevant example. In a number of countries stretching from Nigeria to Malaysia, the state is often so committed to Islamic values that the Koran sometimes forms the basis of the law. Although Americans profess strong religious beliefs, which influence public discourse, religions as organized bodies are blocked from official status due to the First Amendment's requirement for separation of church and state.

Conclusion

Both political parties and interest groups represent important collective vehicles for citizens who share political views. Parties and interest groups are sometimes viewed skeptically from the perspective of democratic theory, as means by which special interests can pursue their goals at the expense of the common good. However, they seem to be a fundamental and inevitable component of democracy, reflecting James Madison's insight that "liberty is to faction what air is to fire." The type, number, and activities of parties and interest groups may vary widely from country to country, but will always conform to the institutions and processes of their countries, while also significantly shaping the politics and government of those countries. The long-term two-party system and the dispersed constellation of interest groups found in the United States are quite unusual in comparative terms, but at this point also integral parts of the American political scene.

Further Reading

- *Political Parties: Old Concepts and New Challenges.* Richard Guther, Jose Ramon Montero, and Juan Linz, Eds. Oxford University Press, New York: 2002.
- *Political Parties and Party Systems.* Alan Ware. Oxford University Press, New York: 1995.
- *First World Interest Groups: A Comparative Perspective.* Clive S. Thomas, Ed. Greenwood Press, Westport, CT: 1993.

Web-Based Exploration Exercise

Visit the Web sites of significant political parties in any two countries outside the United States (a significant party can be defined as one with more than one member of a national legislature). Identify at least one similarity and one difference between the way in which those parties present themselves to voters, via their Website, and compare them with the Democrats and Republicans in the United States. A useful Website for accessing world political parties can be found at <www.gksoft.com/govt/en/parties.html>.

Question for Debate and Discussion

The single-member plurality system and other factors in the United States serve to effectively exclude minor parties from electoral competition. On the whole, is the effect of such exclusion on politics and public policy in the United States positive or negative? What features of other political systems could be adapted to the U.S. political system to expand voter choice among political parties? What might be the disadvantages of such changes?

10
UNCONVENTIONAL
POLITICAL PARTICIPATION

Political participation is often conceptualized as spanning a spectrum from conventional to unconventional modes of behavior. The exact dividing line between the two modes is not always entirely clear and varies from country to country, but the simplest marker is to ask whether a type of political participation can lead to arrest and punishment. In some nondemocratic countries, attempts to organize an election, create a new political party, or even form an interest group might be considered illegal. In more democratic countries, such types of political activity are widely accepted, but other types of more unconventional activity are less tolerated. Peaceful protest marches, demonstrations, and other forms of activism are often highly restricted by the authorities, who may intervene forcefully if traffic is being disrupted or property is being damaged. Almost universally, regardless of whether a country is democratic or nondemocratic, the use of violence to achieve political aims would be met with countermeasures by police or military forces.

Compared with many democracies, conventional political participation in the United States is not particularly robust; as we have seen, the United States has only two major parties, voter turnout rates are quite low, and even interest group activity skews heavily toward the wealthy. Such realities are, to some degree, balanced by a strong tradition of unconventional political participation via social movements and protest activities that originate among outsider groups and target structures of power. In the United States, unconventional political participation, including but not limited to the use of protests and demonstrations, has been most closely associated with marginalized or disempowered groups. Whenever citizens find that their voice is not effectively heard within the political system, they may find it necessary to turn to other means ranging from picketing and demonstrations to violence and even armed insurrection.

Case Study: The Zapatista National Liberation Army in Mexico

Mexico is a country with a long history of demonstrations, protests, and other forms of both violent and nonviolent political activism, usually targeting the long-ruling Revolutionary Institutional Party (PRI). By rigging elections, suppressing opposition, and distributing government funds to win political support, the PRI ruled Mexico for most of the twentieth century. By the 1990s, however, the party's many broken promises, corrupt practices, and authoritarian tactics began to generate serious opposition, especially in crushingly poor rural areas such as the state of Chiapas in the country's far south. In 1992, indigenous groups staged demonstrations to mark the 500th anniversary of Columbus's arrival in the Americas, destroying the statue of a Spanish conquistador in one town. Protests intensified in 1993 when the central government removed traditional protections for peasant landholdings. Then a turning point arrived when Mexico acceded to the North American Free Trade Agreement (NAFTA), which many indigenous peoples viewed as benefiting large agricultural corporations to the detriment of small farmers.

On January 1, 1994, an armed left-wing group calling itself the Zapatista National Liberation Army seized control of four towns in Chiapas and essentially declared war on the PRI and, more broadly, the Mexican government. The initial confrontation was brief, with the Mexican army regaining military control within two weeks. But this proved to be just the opening gambit of the EZLN, whose name invoked the legacy of Emiliano Zapata, the foremost peasant leader of the Mexican Revolution. Reflecting not only the anger of dispossessed peasants but also the anxieties of a country reeling from a series of economic crises, the EZLN became a rallying point for anger at the "democratic dictatorship" of the PRI. Dozens more towns declared themselves to have Zapatista governments and proreform forces in Mexico City and elsewhere rallied to support the EZLN.

Throughout the 1990s, the EZLN proved skillful in building political alliances both inside and outside Mexico, for instance, convoking a forum of indigenous peoples that drew participants from throughout Latin America. The group made especially effective use of the then-burgeoning Internet and other media. In particular, one EZLN leader, a Marxist college professor turned revolutionary known as Subcommandante Marcos, became a folk hero and an iconic figure always seen in a ski mask and usually puffing a pipe. The government signed an agreement with the Zapatistas regarding indigenous rights and culture, but failed to implement it meaningfully. Instead it increased military pressure, covertly supported political assassination, and tacitly approved massacres by paramilitary groups. But each new action by the government drew greater attention from human rights organizations throughout the world, including many on-the-ground observers whose presence disrupted usual patterns of corruption and election rigging.

The activities of the EZLN contributed greatly to the downfall of the PRI in 2000, when for the first time in 72 years the presidency went to the candidate of another party, Vicente Fox. In an extraordinary turnaround, the Zapatistas formed a huge convoy and traveled overland to Mexico City to attempt to promote greater reforms for the impoverished regions of the country. The Zapatistas converged in the zocalo, the city's main plaza, for one of the largest mass demonstrations in Mexican history. One of the group's leaders, Subcommandante Esther in a signature Zapatista ski mask, even delivered an address to Congress. Reflecting the entrenchment of powerful interests in Mexico, however, the Congress passed only weak legislation, leading the EZLN and other groups to continue their struggle for reform.

Political Violence

By the standards of political violence throughout the world, the seizing of villages by the EZLN was a fairly mild event, more a symbolic act than a true armed threat to the Mexican state. Sadly, political violence is far more common and destructive in many other precincts of Latin America. One notable example has been the country of Colombia, which has been torn apart for generations by a complex struggle among at least four players who are sometimes commingled in unpredictable ways. Violent left-wing guerrilla fighters pursuing reform of inequitable land distribution face off against brutal right-wing paramilitary forces bankrolled by wealthy landowners. At the same time, official government forces try to secure control of the country and armed narcotics traffickers seek to ensure profits from the export of cocaine. The citizenry of Colombia have, literally and figuratively, been caught in the crossfire, subject to extortion, kidnappings, assassinations, and massacres. The political system has failed repeatedly to resolve social and economic conflicts and to impose order.

Other regions of Latin America, especially Central America and the Andean nations, have also been prone to similar civil wars, as have parts of Central and West Africa, South and Southeast Asia, and the Middle East, including Iraq most recently. Indeed, in the modern world, civil wars have supplanted international conflicts as the major source of warfare. Such internal battles tend not to meet the older conception of warfare as being time-limited confrontations between two uniformed armies facing off across a battlefield. Rather, they are more likely to involve sporadic episodes of violence and slow, incrementally building conflict occurring on many fronts and using many tactics.

Civil wars are generally of two types: those in which an insurrectionary internal force tries to topple the existing central government (or at least radically alter its policies) and those in which separatist rebels seek autonomy or outright independence for a particular region. Well-established democratic countries such as the United States are largely insulated from the former type of civil war. As long as the democratic system is at least fairly representative of the broad majority of the population and power periodically alternates between competing factions, it is generally far more productive to channel disagreements into politics than into revolutionary conflict to topple the existing regime. Indeed, it has often been said that in democratic systems, "politics is a substitute for warfare." (In one of the world's oldest democracies, Great Britain, this concept was enshrined directly in the architecture of parliament by placing the two opposing sides across an aisle measuring exactly two swords' lengths.)

Of course, even in broadly democratic countries there will always still be some portion of the population—usually the extreme left or right wings—who believe that they cannot achieve their goals through the existing structures of the state and who may challenge the legitimacy of the state itself. Such extremists can certainly be deadly in their actions; a compelling example in the United States was the Oklahoma City bombing in 1995 in which the right-wing ideologue Timothy McVeigh bombed a federal office building to strike a blow against what he saw as a tyrannical U.S. government. Acts of political violence have also originated from the left in the United States, notably in the 1960s and 1970s, when armed revolutionary factions, such as The Weathermen, radicalized by the Vietnam War, planted bombs in a string of government facilities.

While such fringe elements may gain media attention, and perhaps some small number of new adherents, their potential base of support is far too narrow to build or sustain the kind of force that could challenge the power of the state. Further, most democratic—and no small number of nondemocratic countries—have formidable means at their disposal to crush any nascent insurgency, ranging from police forces to intelligence agencies to the military. It is thus mostly countries with comparatively weak governments (such as in Colombia) that have trouble exerting control over mountainous or dense jungle terrain, in which struggles for control of the state ever have the opportunity to even begin.

The second kind of civil war, focused on achieving independence for a particular geographic region, is more common. When a portion of a country wishes to territorially secede from an established country and become a new independent state, central authorities tend to reflexively resist. Sometimes, the central authorities may be concerned about the loss of some economic resource. Current debates over the possible secession of Kurdistan from Iraq, for instance, are largely concerned with which entity would be left with control of the revenue-generating Kirkuk oilfields. Other times, the central authorities fear that a successful secession might set a damaging precedent, spurring other regions to break free of centralized control and threatening territorial integrity, historic continuity, and national honor of the state. This explains in part the brutal lengths to which the Kremlin has gone to suppress Chechen rebels, given that there are more than a hundred non-Russian ethnic groups living within the boundaries of the Russian Federation.

As in Kurdistan and Chechnya, separatism often arises among groups that are distinct from the national majority in terms of ethnicity, religion, language, or some other cultural or historical factor, and consider themselves oppressed on the basis of that difference. Separatist-oriented civil conflict can be hard for even democratic countries to resolve because minorities are likely to feel outnumbered and poorly represented in the political system. Even in vigorously democratic and usually quiescent Canada, Quebec separatism took a violent turn in 1970 with the assassination of a provincial cabinet member, one of only two political killings in the country's history and the first in over a century. More generally, separatist groups can survive if they have at least the implicit support and cooperation of the local population, giving them a basis for sustained agitation against the state. And they are likely to have the advantage of being in a defensive rather than an offensive mode, seeking to consolidate local control rather than wrest power over the entire country from national authorities.

A number of the longest running conflicts within established democracies relate to separatist impulses among small minority groups. Two of the most intense modern separatist conflicts in post-World War II Europe involved the attempts of the Irish Republican Army (IRA) to force the British out of Northern Ireland, and the Basque Homeland and Freedom (ETA) group to seek separation of ethnically Basque territories from Spain. The IRA essentially sought to bring the British-controlled four northernmost Irish counties into the independent Republic of Ireland, arguing that Northern Irish Catholics were being persecuted by the Protestant majority. The ETA movement emerged in opposition to the long suppression of the highly distinctive Basque culture and language under the regime of Spanish dictator Francisco Franco. Both movements used a wide variety of bombings, terror threats, and assassinations, up to and including foiled plots against the lives of the British and Spanish monarchs.

After decades of strife and conflict, however, both insurgencies seemed to largely come to a halt in the early 2000s through the decidedly peaceful and democratic means of devolving power. London devolved power to a Northern Irish government, while Madrid essentially reinterpreted its constitution to offer quasi-autonomy to the Basques. In both cases, insurgents renounced violence, disarmed and demobilized, and tentatively joined the political process. At the same time, devolution of power appears to also have defused separationist impulses in Scotland and Wales in Britain, as well as in Catalonia in Spain. Notably, this potentially peaceful outcome has required no actual changes in territory or sovereignty, although the matter was undoubtedly helped by the participation of Britain, Ireland, and Spain in the transnational European Union, which has made old territorial disputes seem less relevant.

In broad historical terms, the United States is no stranger to separatist civil war, of course. Remarkably, however, the United States has not witnessed any large-scale violent insurrections on its soil since 1865. This can partly be traced to memories of the sheer trauma of the U.S. Civil War, which constitutes the major national tragedy of American history and remains prominent in the national consciousness. The U.S. Civil War also resolved lingering constitutional questions about the proper relationship of the U.S. states to the national government, providing legitimacy to the idea that the national government is clearly supreme and that the union is indivisible. But the successful avoidance of further separatism in the United States has also been the result of pragmatic political compromises of the kind that were not reached in time to avert the Civil War. Thus in the period after the end of Reconstruction in 1877, the southern states were returned to self-government through a negotiated settlement. Part of the price of peace, however, was that the southern states were allowed to enforce a system of racial segregation—in fact, outright subordination—of African Americans.

This pragmatic but unprincipled compromise may have resolved one political problem, but it prolonged another. It is noteworthy that the closest that any region of the country has come to outright rebellion since 1865 was also in the states of the former Confederacy. During the Civil Rights Movement of the 1950s and 1960s, both the population at large and elected officials mounted massive resistance to the racial desegregation ordered by the courts. Occasionally, the federal government had to resort to force in several southern states, such as the use of federal troops to integrate the high school in Little Rock, Arkansas, although the Civil Rights Era never developed into anything approaching outright armed conflict. Indeed, in many ways the country once again reached a negotiated solution in the 1980s and 1990s. Officially sanctioned racial segregation of neighborhoods, workplaces, and schools was ended. But attempts to reach full integration of housing, employment, and education were largely abandoned, leaving in place striking gaps in socioeconomic status and life opportunities between whites and people of color.

Such an incomplete reckoning with the legacy of racism in the United States has contributed to what is arguably the principal form of political violence in the United States today. Observers disagree about whether to call such episodes riots, rebellions, urban insurrections, or simple mob violence. But their usual manifestation is a long-simmering anger among poor, inner-city, racial, and ethnic minority groups, that explodes in a spontaneous burst of street violence, arson, looting, and other forms of lawlessness. Such events occurred in cities such as Newark and Detroit in the late 1960s, for instance, sparked by the news that the Rev. Martin Luther King, Jr., had been assassinated. By far the most prominent recent example in the United States occurred in Los Angeles in 1992 when the South Central neighborhood experienced three days of violence following the acquittal of four members of the L.A. Police Department accused of brutalizing a black motorist. The L.A. Riots were forms of political violence in a different way than, say, the coordinated bombings by the Weathermen or by Timothy McVeigh in that they were unplanned and unorganized and did not seek to advance a particular political goal. However, they were a reaction to the long-term grievances of populations who felt themselves to be marginalized by an unresponsive political system and oppressed by the brutal tactics of the L.A. Police Department.

Such bursts of violence are far from uniquely American. Among democracies, France offers archetypal examples of spontaneous, often violent urban unrest, given both its revolutionary tradition and its strong conception of every citizen relating directly to the state without group intermediaries. In late 2005 in the slums on the outskirts of Paris, for instance, groups of unemployed youths of North African descent torched cars and damaged property to protest their sense of exclusion from full participation in French society. Spontaneous uprisings of this type certainly attract attention to an issue, and may win some short-term concessions from the government, but their longer-term effectiveness is very much subject to doubt. The end result of such episodes seems often to be the destruction of the rioters' own neighborhoods, the devastation of local economies, increased pressure on the part of police and government, and the bolstering of law-and-order advocates in the next election cycle.

Peaceful Protest

If political violence is always considered a form of unconventional political participation, peaceful protest straddles the line between the conventional and unconventional. Peaceful protest may be sporadic or sustained, spontaneous or organized, but its goal is not to use force to enact change but rather to bring pressure to bear on the political establishment to enact reform. The example of the EZLN in Mexico is particularly interesting because it represents the coalescence of scattered groups of protestors into an armed force, which then transformed itself into a mostly peaceful protest movement. Despite a continued rhetoric of militancy and the symbolic maintaining of an armed presence, the Zapatistas present far less of a military challenge to the Mexican government than a political one. In reality, they pose no threat of fomenting secession in Chiapas state, much less of seizing control of the Mexican state. But as attested to by their dramatic march on Mexico City, their mass rally in the city's main square, and their continued high profile on the Internet and in various other media, the Zapatistas have helped to promote the democratization of the country.

In countries with repressive governments, spontaneous protest activities may occur from time to time but the police and other government forces are usually able to curb the emergence of full-scale movements. Such a scattered approach still tends to be common in nondemocratic countries in which the citizens may hold targeted demonstrations to air a particular grievance, but then are prevented by the police or other authorities from forming into organized protest groups. For instance, landless farmers, displaced villagers, and others excluded from the advance of affluence in China regularly picket and demonstrate, but the government then uses arrests, threats, or economic incentives to defuse the situation. While such repression can quell protest in the short term, it runs the risk of bottling up discontent, which can explode into revolutionary conditions, as happened with the ousting of such dictators as the Shah of Iran in 1979 and President Fidel Marcos of the Philippines in 1986. By contrast, nonviolent social movements, when allowed to function freely, can serve as safety-valves for democracy, providing a forum within which grievances can be aired and demands made for reform.

With its comparatively open society, the United States has been a particularly fertile home for sustained and organized protest movements; examples stretch back to antislavery abolitionists, suffragettes seeking the right to vote for women, the antialcohol prohibitionists, and labor union activists. The modern prototype of a protest movement in the United States is the African-American Civil Rights Movement, which itself drew upon and applied lessons learned during the struggle for the independence of India led by Mohandas K. Gandhi. The Civil Rights Movement pioneered tactics including boycotts of segregated bus services, sit-ins at lunch counters that refused to serve black customers, pickets and demonstrations up to and including a mass march on Washington, and jail-ins designed to force authorities to arrest so many protestors as to strain their capacity to function. These and other tactics of nonviolent civil disobedience are especially well suited for use by social groups that are disadvantaged and discriminated against, but who live within countries that are democratic enough to allow some latitude for citizen initiative.

Waves of successive protest movements have emerged in the United States and other democratic countries since the 1960s. Perhaps because of the strength of group identities in the United States, American protest movements have tended to be based around stable, long-term sources of identity such as gender, sexual orientation, and physical disability. Such U.S.-initiated movements have often had a major influence on protest politics among such groups around the world. For example, the many branches of the global movement for gay and lesbian equality almost all trace their roots to three days of rioting in New York City in June 1969, which ensued after police raided a gay bar called the Stonewall Inn. Every June, in commemoration of the Stonewall Riots, hundreds of gay and lesbian communities throughout the world hold "pride marches," lively parades held on the main thoroughfares of major cities that bring people "out of the closet" and into public view while demonstrating significant numbers of supporters. Similarly, AIDS activism as a social movement also traces its roots to New York City, where in 1987 the local gay community formed the direct-action protest group ACT UP, which in turn spawned chapters and affiliated organizations across the country and around the world.

Compared with other countries, protest politics in the United States has often been built around group identities and thus less around broad ideologies or issues that affect the nation or world at large. For instance, environmental activism has been less extensive and coherent in the United States than in Western Europe, where green movements have become so well developed that they have evolved into full-scale political parties. Similarly, the nuclear-disarmament movement of the 1980s and subsequent peace movements garnered far more support in European countries than they ever did in the United States, except perhaps during times when American troops are actually in combat. One of the most recent broad protest movements in the United States, the proimmigrant demonstrations which swept the country in 2006, appear in retrospect to have been mostly based in Latino immigrant communities rather than based on broader social solidarities or rooted in larger ideological concerns. Even protest among students, so influential in other countries, is relatively muted, with most American college students appearing to have little interest in large-scale challenges to the government or to social norms. Rather, the reigning paradigm of multiculturalism at American universities seems to have the effect of channeling student activism toward protest based on group-level identities of gender, race, or ethnicity rather than broader ideological issues.

Aside from a few eras, such as the labor unrest of the 1930s, class-based protest movements have also not been very central to American history. Compared with the wealthy nations of Europe, the United States has seen much less class warfare calling for high tax rates to allow for massive income redistribution or for heavy government regulation of the workplace, such as by offering job guarantees. Rather, American labor unions have focused on narrower employment issues such as wages and benefits. Partly as a result, a disproportionate number of Americans continue to live in or near poverty, benefiting little from the economic dynamism that has made the United States the wealthiest country in the world. Even traumatic events such as the aftermath of Hurricane Katrina in 2005, which vividly exposed the vulnerability of the poor and the limited scope of government services for them, appear to have done little to spur sustained protest or activism on behalf of poverty reduction. In fact, no serious attempt at reducing poverty has been undertaken in the United States since the mid-1960s, with economic inequality growing steadily since that time.

The lack of class-based protest in the United States appears to be rooted in longer-term historical factors that have prevented the development of a high degree of class consciousness and the resulting cultivation of socialism as a political ideology. One line of reasoning argues that a commitment to socialism did not emerge in the United States because there was never an entrenched upper class in the United States as there was in Europe, where feudal aristocracies struggled throughout the nineteenth century to maintain their traditional wealth and power. Absent such pitched class struggle, the United States had no need for a counterbalancing degree of mobilization among ordinary people, such as through the mass labor movement. Another, complementary, line of argument focuses on the opportunities for social mobility present in the dynamic American economy, in which individuals could rise and fall on their own initiative, such as by opening their own small businesses or joining the westward migration. The perception that the U.S. system offered opportunities for individual advancement tended to breed envy rather than anger of those higher up the socioeconomic ladder. Poor and working class people did not so much want to displace the wealthy as to emulate them.

Another important factor suppressing class-based protest in the United States is the separation of government and the economy into largely separate spheres. The comparatively low levels of government involvement in and regulation of the U.S. economy simply make it less productive to carry out political protests in pursuit of economic goals. When governments own or control large sectors of the economy, protestors know where to direct their grievances, but the more decentralized, market-based economy of the United States offers fewer clear-cut targets to protestors. As noted in the previous chapter, labor unions in the United States have never had the level of power they possess in Europe, and union membership in the United States has been declining for decades. What class-based protest can be seen in the United States is often refracted through other group identities, such as concerns about the wage disparities between men and women or the difficulties facing ethnic and racial minorities.

Conclusion

Democracy tends to direct citizen input into conventional modes of political participation such as voting and involvement with political parties and interest groups. Unconventional means of participation can also have an impact on politics, however. At their best they serve as additional vehicles for democracy, but at their worst can create instability and unrest. Since the American Civil War, the United States has largely avoided political violence on its territory although there have been sporadic riots, uprisings, and other isolated incidents. Most unconventional participation takes the form of peaceful protest, particularly with regard to the grievances of particular groups rather than challenges to the state or the basic order of society.

Further Reading

- *Comparative Perspectives on Social Movements: Political Opportunities, Mobilizing Structures, and Cultural Framings.* Doug McAdam, John D. McCarthy and Meyer N. Zald, Eds. Cambridge University Press, New York: 1996.
- *Social Movements, Political Violence, and the State.* Donatella Della Porta. Cambridge University Press, New York: 1996.

- *Challenging the Political Order: New Social and Political Movements in Western Democracies.* Russell J. Dalton and Mandred Kuechler, Eds. Oxford University Press, New York: 1990.

Web-Based Exploration Exercise

Visit the Web sites of any three social movements in the world. Identify at least one of their issues and one of their tactics, and discuss the extent to which these issues and tactics would be relevant to the context of the United States. A directory of world social movements can be found at <http://social-movements.org>.

Question for Debate and Discussion

Protest politics is a common activity in the U.S. political system. What dimensions of the U.S. political system may help to channel citizens toward protest politics? What reforms could be introduced from other political systems that might reduce the occurrence of protest politics in the United States?

11

PUBLIC OPINION AND POLITICAL VALUES

Unlike voting behavior, protest actions, or the activities of political parties and interest groups, public opinion is not in itself a form of political participation. However, the views of the public on a range of issues, and the political values that undergird those views, greatly influence other forms of political behavior. These help to determine, for instance, for whom citizens vote, whether they engage in other political activities, or whether they vote at all. Further, in an era of near-constant polling of every type, public opinion surveys have become a de facto form of political participation, albeit a passive one based on the initiative of newspapers, government officials, and other actors who collect information from the mass public. This is especially true in countries, such as the United States, with vigorous free presses and frequent competitive elections. But even closed, authoritarian governments must take care to keep the pulse of public opinion, if only to figure out how to promote the cooperation and dampen the resistance of their populations.

In the short run, public opinion can be volatile and appear unstable. Responses to public opinion polls vary over time and according to specific circumstances. For instance, after the September 11 terrorist attacks, concerns about security rose sharply in U.S. polls; likewise, financial worries routinely increase in times of economic recession. Such shifts are fairly easily explained and common among populations around the world. Of greater interest for present purposes are broader and deeper patterns of beliefs, values, and opinions in the United States, and how those compare with other countries.

It is notoriously difficult to generalize about the political opinions held by any group, much less by entire countries. Indeed, the very attempt to identify and define the political culture of a country runs the risk of descending into overly broad judgments and casual stereotyping, and it certainly can never represent the views of every member of that country. Thus, for instance, the oft-noted tendency of the Japanese to be group-oriented and Americans to be individualists obscures the fact that Japanese are, of course, all individuals and that Americans gather together in groups of all types. To say that people in Iran support the commingling of religion and government while those in the United States prefer the separation of church and state overlooks those Iranians who might prefer a more secular state and those Americans who are ready to embrace theocracy. But over time and across surveys, it does become possible to generalize about the values, beliefs, and opinions of countries in the aggregate, and to see how they are similar to and different from other countries.

Case Study: The World Values Survey and the Inglehart Values Map

One of the largest, most comprehensive, and most influential, studies of comparative political values and public opinion is the World Values Survey, led by the political scientist Ronald Inglehart and colleagues in the 1990s. Between 1990 and 1993, with several follow-up studies since then, the World Values Survey asked some 350 questions of thousands of respondents in dozens of countries representing 70 percent of the world's population. The societies varied widely in terms of geography, culture, politics, and economics, ranging from democratic to authoritarian regimes, from laissez-faire capitalist to central-directed socialist economies, from the wealthiest to some of the poorest countries. The survey's often-cited results provide a basis for standardized examination of dozens of topics relating to politics, economics, and social issues.

The single most compelling product of the World Values Survey has come to be known as the Inglehardt Values Map. (The map, and accompanying discussion, can be accessed at <www.worldvaluessurvey.com/library/set_illustrations.html>) Depending upon their responses to particular questions, the forty societies in the study are placed on the map according to an X coordinate on the horizontal axis and a Y coordinate on the vertical axis. The X coordinate is fairly straightforward, relating to *survival* values (emphasizing the struggle for economic and physical security) versus *well-being* values (focusing on more subjective standards of self-expression and quality of life).

The Y coordinate refers to the source of authority cited by the respondents in their answers: whether it was traditional or secular–rational. Those who were on the traditional side cited obedience to religious authority and strong adherence to standard of behavior expected by family, communal, and national ties. As might be expected, the traditionalists believe in absolute standards of morality; uphold traditional views of divorce, abortion, euthanasia, and related social issues; and are highly nationalistic. Those on the secular–rational side embody the opposite set of values, stressing individual achievement and personal liberty with a heavy emphasis on the role of an active state and comparatively less deference to the expectations of religion, families, or communities.

The remarkable result of the mapping of the forty societies provides visual confirmation that they cluster together in highly predictable ways. The Inglehart Values Map strongly suggests that the political values held by people around the world are closely related to their specific geographic, historic, economic, and religious experiences and traditions. For instance, the countries of South Asia, Latin America, and Africa each form into distinctive clusters, and all three regions—representing the survey's sample from the developing world—strongly advocate traditional values over secular–rational values. Similarly, the Confucian countries of East Asia, the formerly Communist countries of Eastern Europe, the traditionally Catholic countries of Europe, and the traditionally Protestant countries of Europe all also cluster together, generally favoring secular–rational authority over traditional authority.

As might be expected on the survival vs. well-being dimension, the poorer countries of the world reflect a much greater emphasis on survival than the wealthier countries, with the countries of Africa and South Asia nearly all emphasizing fundamental economic and physical security. Populations of formerly Communist countries also tend to heavily emphasize survival values, even though most are objectively wealthier than countries in the developing world. The economic and political uncertainty and upheaval of the 1990s in Eastern Europe and the former Soviet Union, including the loss of the cradle-to-grave social programs provided by Communism, seem to have raised great anxieties about physical and economic security. Latin American countries, many of which are somewhat wealthier than some African and Asian countries, modestly veer in the direction of well-being values. Western European countries all fit clearly on the self-expression side of the map.

So where does the United States fit into all of this? On the survival versus well-being values—essentially the economic dimension—the United States is much like the other countries of the wealthy world, placing right in the middle of the European countries and closest to such other wealthy nations as Austria, Switzerland, Iceland, and Norway. Most Americans, like Western Europeans, are not consumed with the question of how they will get by on a day-to-day basis, but focus instead on quality-of-life issues.

Strikingly, however, the United States rates traditional sources of authority more highly than *any* other established wealthy country and more highly than all but three countries of the developed world (the devoutly Catholic and traditionally poor European nations of Ireland, Poland, and Portugal). On the spectrum of traditional values versus secular–rational values, the United States places midway between the two polar opposites of Japan and El Salvador; its position on the map puts the U.S. rather far from most of the countries of Europe and closest to Uruguay, Romania, India, and Vietnam. When both axes are considered, the United States places into a clear cluster of English-speaking countries alongside Australia, Canada, and New Zealand, with Britain and Ireland slightly further away. This clustering clearly suggests a significant role for history, culture, geography, legal inheritance, and even language in the making of public opinion.

United States Public Opinion in Comparative Perspective

As the World Values Survey suggests, the United States is among the most typical of developed nations in some ways and at the same time among the most atypical in other ways. The ways in which the United States is typical—its emphasis on well-being values over survival values—are fairly easily explained and unsurprising. Inglehart and his colleagues refer to the positioning of the United States—and virtually all other countries of the developed world—as reflecting a shift from industrial to postindustrial societies. The unprecedented affluence of the developed world has meant that most people do not find basic material existence needs to be more compelling than "postmaterial" values such as control over one's work circumstances, the importance of leisure pursuits, and general life satisfaction. The economies of the developed world are so prosperous that they provide many opportunities for jobs that pay well enough to satisfy basic human needs. The existence of a social safety net for those in economic hardship further allows most people in Europe and North America to avoid being preoccupied with simple survival. Given this basic security, people's minds naturally gravitate to higher-order concerns such as psychological well being, personal fulfillment, and opportunities for self-expression.

Income inequality certainly continues to persist in the developed world in general, and in the United States in particular. However, only the most unfortunate citizens in the developed countries—such as the homeless—experience levels of material deprivation comparable with those of great masses of people in the developing world. That is to say, the poor in Western Europe or North America may experience relative deprivation in areas such as having substandard education, shoddy housing, and limited disposable income. But, despite the use of the same word, poverty in the United States is categorically different from poverty in a developing world context. This is made manifest by the willingness, even eagerness, of millions of undocumented immigrants to leave their own countries to occupy even the lowest rung of the socioeconomic ladder in the developed world. Mexicans coming to the United States, Algerians moving to France, Turks arriving in Germany, or Vietnamese relocating to Australia—all of these offer striking testimony to the immensity of the disparities between the poor and rich countries of the world.

While it is not difficult to explain why Americans are like others in the developed world with regard to well-being issues, it is rather more challenging to explain the ways in which Americans are unlike those in other wealthy democratic nations. As noted above, the United States emphasizes traditional over secular–rational values more highly than almost any other developed nation. To some extent, this difference should not be overstated; Americans are only midway on this scale and are notably more secular–rational than the peoples of nearly all developing countries. And significant swathes of the American population, mostly registered Democrats and ideological liberals, hold views not too far removed from the European mainstream. Still, some of these differences are real enough to offer some sharp contrasts with Western European and other developed countries, and often are the basis for miscommunication and mistrust between the United States and its allies. Many of these issues have been cogently analyzed through various surveys conducted by the Pew Global Attitudes Project (<www.pewglobal.org>), whose data form the basis of the discussion below. United States public opinion and political values particularly stand out in three areas: religiosity and moral values informed by religion, belief in self-reliance over big government, and strong patriotism and national pride.

Religiosity

As might be expected from the Inglehart Values Map, Americans are strikingly more religious than people in most other developed countries. In fact, the United States is the *only* country in the world that is democratic, wealthy, and highly religious, making for a truly anomalous combination. In the United States, 94 percent of the population indicates a belief in God, compared with 61 percent in Britain and 50 percent in Germany. Most Americans (58 percent) state that a belief in God is necessary for a person to be moral; only 30 percent of Canadians and 13 percent of French agree; a similar majority of Americans (59 percent) call religion very important in the lives, while 27 percent of Italians and 21 percent of Germans hold this view. Rates of membership in organized religious bodies and attendance at worship services are also higher in the United States than anywhere else in the western world.

The religiosity of Americans has some clear impact on their opinions on a variety of issues. Compared with people in other developed countries, Americans are generally more likely to view prostitution, abortion, suicide, and euthanasia as being never justifiable, although the gaps are not always huge. Just 51 percent of Americans agree that homosexuality should be accepted by society, compared with 74 percent of British and 83 percent of Germans. While Americans may be more progressive on these social issues than most developing-world populations, the relative prudishness of Americans is an object of some wonderment and even scorn on the part of Europeans. For instance, the idea that an American president could be threatened with removal from office for a sexual dalliance with a young woman baffled many in Europe; as one American comedian noted at the time, the French would probably impeach their president if it were discovered that he didn't have a mistress. And, indeed, when former French President Francois Mitterand died, his burial was attended by his wife and their sons as well as his long-term mistress and their grown daughter. Mitterand, who was elected twice as president, was also an openly avowed atheist, a religious sensibility that a majority of Americans say would disqualify someone from their vote for U.S. president.

Many of the religious and moral issues that are the subject of heated debate in the United States have been largely resolved in Western Europe. Access to abortion services, contraception, and comprehensive sex education is largely uncontroversial. Assisted suicide for the terminally ill, same-sex marriage, and use of soft drugs such as marijuana are less universally embraced, but there is a strong, clear trend toward broader acceptance of these issues. Some issues that regularly arise in American politics debate—such as whether to teach evolution, creationism, "intelligent design," or all of these in public schools—would be considered akin to debating flat-earth theories in most of Europe.

Thus, it is clear that Americans are quite anomalous on religion when compared with the populations of most other developed nations. In fact, however, it is *those* nations that are anomalous when viewed in world context: 80 to 97 percent of respondents from fourteen African and South Asian countries rated religion as very important, while figures for most South American respondents were between 60 and 80 percent. Also, European populations are also much less religious than they were even two generations ago, with their withdrawal from religion occurring mostly since about World War II.

Thus, the real question may not be why Americans are religious, but why Europeans have become so secularized in recent decades. The answer in most of the formerly Communist countries of Central and Eastern Europe seems fairly clear cut—forty years under the sway of authoritarian governments that discouraged religion and promoted atheism have disrupted traditional patterns of religious devotion in most, although not all, places. The decline of religion in most of Western Europe—and also in other Western countries such as Canada, Australia, and New Zealand—appears rather more challenging to explain.

One line of reasoning holds that the rise of robust government welfare programs in Western countries undermined the traditional role of religious bodies in distributing charity. From this perspective, church attendance declined as people needed neither the material resources formerly distributed by churches nor, amid postwar conditions of peace and prosperity, the spiritual comfort that religion can provide. In the United States, by contrast, nongovernmental actors, and in particular religious institutions, still play a major role in providing services. It is also striking that some of the most ardently religious communities in the United States are those that still face social and economic difficulties, notably African Americans. Likewise, the most thoroughly secularized European countries, those in the Nordic countries, also have the most elaborate social welfare systems.

Another line of reasoning argues that the established, state-supported churches in many of those countries were stodgy and dull compared with the profusion of religious denominations within the United States. Official churches that in the nineteenth and early twentieth centuries were supported by tax dollars, or other types of public support, did not need to fill the pews in order to survive. Over time, they grew to be inward-looking and uninspiring, a drab obligation on occasions such as weddings and funerals rather than a vital part of people's lives. The United States, by contrast, was founded by many people who were seeking liberty from such hidebound and oppressive established churches, and as such a wall of separation was introduced between church and state by the First Amendment. The result was a far more competitive market in the United States, where many different religious traditions developed, emphasizing distinctive theological perspectives and worship styles and thus engaging a broader swath of society. The presence of so many different religious bodies has also fostered a spirit of tolerance in the United States, in which many people hold their own beliefs strongly but respect the rights of others to have different religious convictions (as long as they have religious convictions of some sort).

On religious, social, and moral issues in the United States, there are definitely also libertarian strains that prefer the noninterference of government in the people's personal lives, as well as some secular and progressive strains whose views are not dissimilar from those of Western Europe, including some elements of the media and educational elite. Indeed, one American political commentator, Fox News's Bill O'Reilly, has built a career on condemning "secular progressives" in the United States and finds himself with the type of huge, receptive audience that would be unthinkable in most developed countries.

Self-Reliance and Skepticism about Big Government

Another strikingly consistent finding in comparative public opinion polling is that Americans hold beliefs in self-reliance and skepticism of big government that are among the highest in the developed world. Just 32 percent of Americans agree with the statement that "success in life is determined by forces outside our control," compared with 68 percent of Germans, 66 percent of Italians, and 48 percent of British. When asked whether government should leave people alone to pursue their own goals or should offer guarantees to everyone in need, 58 percent of Americans endorsed self-determination versus 43 percent of Canadians, 36 percent of French, and 24 percent of Italians.

Such preference for individual liberty over societal equality is a long-term and familiar finding in the study of American political culture. Although they are often discussed together, liberty and equality actually in many ways can be in tension. People have greatly different endowments in terms of intelligence, skills, ambition, emotional maturity, and all the other characteristics that shape their job success and life circumstances. Different individuals will also bring various resources and life experiences from their environments, such as whether they received a solid education, quality health care, or good job training. And people with characteristics that evoke prejudice, such as their race, ethnicity, or gender, among those in positions of power, may also find their chances in life curtailed. Given these many individual and environmental differences, the more that a society focuses on individual liberty, the more people will find themselves under conditions of inequality of income, life chances, and overall options in the "pursuit of happiness" identified as a national goal in the Declaration of Independence. Conversely, the more that government promotes equality, the less liberty may be enjoyed by the population at large, who are likely to be heavily taxed to provide social services for the poor, to find their business activities heavily regulated by government, or to find that they must associate with groups they may dislike, at least in the public sphere.

Compared with most developed nations, the United States has had a modest commitment to promoting socioeconomic equality. Based on higher tax rates and control of a higher percentage of overall gross national product, most European countries provide their poor with far more generous income transfers and supportive services such as subsidized rent and supplemental income. University tuition is often free or at very low cost, and access to health care is universal. The minimum wage can be more than double its level in the United States, while unemployment and disability compensation is provided at a higher rate and for a longer period of time—sometimes indefinitely. Many European workers also have far more job security, a shorter work week, longer vacations, and fully paid parental leaves to care of a newborn, for a year or longer, as opposed to unpaid twelve-week leaves in the United States. Many Americans were baffled when French students stormed the streets of Paris in 2006 because of a law that would have allowed employers to more easily fire employees under age twenty-five, which hardly sounds radical to American ears. Framed as an assault on employment guarantees, however, the protests quickly succeeded and the French government withdrew the pending bill.

Yet there was a reason that the French government pursued legislation to give employers greater flexibility in hiring and firing personnel. Many European welfare states find themselves with moribund economies experiencing unimpressive growth rates and unable to produce enough good jobs for populations that are highly educated and have a strong sense of entitlement. Further, government ownership or control of large portions of the market for utilities, communication, transportation, housing, and other sectors is both expensive and inefficient. By comparison, the light touch of government in the United States and relatively low tax rates have fueled impressive economic growth, promoted low unemployment rates, and opened up opportunities for entrepreneurship and individual success. American businesses have far greater flexibility to offer innovations and meet the changing demands of the marketplace, even when that means wholesale layoffs or the slashing of fringe benefits provided to workers. Similarly, U.S. public policy tends to heavily apply private-sector-oriented solutions, such as helping the poor with tax credits rather than direct subsidies or providing vouchers for private housing rather than constructing and managing extensive public housing complexes. Collectively, such promarket policies have promoted greater overall wealth and prosperity in the United States, although it is dispersed in extremely unequal patterns.

Why does the United States have such a greater regard for self-reliance and a skepticism of big government? Some commentators have pointed to the legacy of racial and ethnic divisions in the United States, which traditionally did not exist in the much more homogenous states of Europe. Because poverty is concentrated among ethnic and racial minority groups, it is argued, the white majority has been more willing to dismiss poverty as a problem of others rather than their concern. In fact, many government welfare programs introduced as part of the New Deal were deliberately structured in ways that disadvantaged African Americans. The heavy emphasis on racial and ethnic divisions in the United States has also dampened the development of class cohesion among working-class whites, blacks, Latinos, and other groups, thus weakening the ability of the labor unions to press for income redistribution. Rather than tackle persistent problems of social and economic disadvantage in a serious way, the United States has increased its prison population 500 percent over the past thirty years, now incarcerating a higher percentage of its population than any other country in the world and drastically more than any other established democracy. The prison population is heavily composed of impoverished and poorly educated African-American and Latino men, who together represent about 12 percent of the U.S. population but more than 60 percent of those incarcerated in prison.

A very different line of argumentation about small government in the United States focuses on the role of defense spending by the United States, especially during the Cold War between 1947 and 1991. Protected under the nuclear shield of the United States, the countries of Western Europe paid relatively little for their own defense and were able to redirect their tax revenues toward building welfare states. In the aftermath of World War II, most European countries were burdened by destruction and deprivation, even as they found themselves withdrawing from their overseas empires and relegated to marginal status in the conflict between two superpowers. As such, European governments' main claim to legitimacy shifted from military prowess and national glory to the improvement of their citizens' everyday life circumstances, leading to the flourishing of the welfare state. The United States, strapped with the leading role in the Western military alliance, could not also afford to develop its social programs—consider the collapse of the mid-1960s War on Poverty under the weight of spending on the Vietnam War. Then, in a vicious circle, Americans have tended to see little of the return on their investment in their daily lives that is so obvious to European taxpayers, generating further hostility toward any attempt to raise taxes in the United States.

The single most influential line of reasoning about the American preference for self-reliance can be characterized as the settler–frontier–immigration thesis. Although each of these strands is a distinct part of the American experience, collectively they created a country in which opportunities for self-reinvention and individual success were limited only by each person's own efforts. Many early setters had fled from repressive kings and clerics and, thus, were only too glad to be free of government and church meddling in their lives. By virtue of circumstance, the earliest settlers were also left almost entirely to their own devices, with no preexisting government to either help them or hinder them. Social mobility became the norm: with no indigenous aristocratic hierarchy held over from feudalism, individuals were free to improve upon the circumstances of their birth. Much the same was true for those who participated in the subsequent nineteenth century westward migration, which came to be viewed as an all-purpose solution to poverty: if things were bad, you could always build your own fortune by moving west. Finally, the self-reliance mentality was perpetuated among the huge waves of southern and eastern European immigrants who entered the country between the 1880s and 1920s. Many of these "tired, poor, huddled masses" were attracted to the United States as the land of opportunity where hard work and diligence could secure a better future, particularly for the next generation. For all of these and other reasons, as discussed further in Chapter 10, class conflict and the ideology associated with it—socialism—have never become strongly established in the United States.

Taken together, the settler–frontier–immigration experience promoted a political culture that views government as more of a threat to individual liberty than its guarantor. This has been a long-term, even permanent feature of American political thought from the Revolutionary Era, when Thomas Jefferson declared, "that government is best that governs least," to the 1980s when Ronald Reagan famously proclaimed that "government is not the solution; it is the problem." At the same time, the United States developed a robust voluntary sector, or civil society, with a diverse array of private associations, religious bodies, and for-profit businesses providing many of the services for which Europeans look to their governments. Even the New Deal of the 1930s, which dramatically expanded the role of the federal government in the economy, was more of an attempt to save capitalism from its own excesses than to promote socialism.

Still another factor is that, ideologically, the United States was born out of a revolution and was based on the rejection of the power of the state in favor of individual liberty. The founders of the American republic were almost fanatical about the need to avoid tyranny, or the excesssive power of government over the individual. On this score, Canadian history offers an intriguing what-if case study in the development of American political culture. Both countries had some-what similar experiences of European settlement, westward migra-tion, and subsequent waves of immigration. However, Canada never experienced a revolution, but has undergone slow evolutionary political change. Whereas the American Declaration of Independence called for "life, liberty, and the pursuit of happiness," the Canadian founding documents of 1867 promised "peace, order, and good government."

Rather than structuring their politics to overthrow monarchy and defend against tyranny, Canadians developed a quieter political culture of deference to rightful authority and concern for the common good. Even as the Canadian federation expanded toward the Pacific Ocean, Canada never really experienced a "Wild West." Instead, its govern-ment authority—best symbolized by the Royal Canadian Mounted Police, often called the "Mounties"—accompanied or even preceded westward migrants. Today, Canadian political culture stands some-where halfway between that of the United States and Western Europe in public opinion polls. Canadians are less devout than Americans but more religiously adherent than Europeans. They demonstrate less of a commitment to socialism than their major colonizers, Britain and France, but more support than is found in the United States for activist government. Canadians (at least English speakers) and Americans—shaped by so many similar circumstances and cross-border influences—are on the whole much more like each other than they are like any other peoples. Yet from same-sex marriage to the decriminalization of marijuana to its signature national health care system, Canadian public policy remains quite distinct from that found in the United States.

Patriotism and National Pride

Finally, Americans reveal levels of national pride and patriotic fervor much more like peoples in the developing world than in the developed world. When asked if they are "very proud" to be citizens of their countries, 71 percent of Americans agreed, but only 45 percent of British and 38 percent of French and Italians. (By contrast, 87 percent of Filipinos, 72 percent of Nigerians, and 67 percent of Indians shared this sense of national pride.) Comparatively speaking, Americans appear to have a clear sense of where they are in the world, and that is at the top. The enormity of the American economy, the power of the American military, the influence of American political ideas, the popularity of American films, television and music—all of these lead many Americans to reflexively assume their country and the culture to be "the best." Even before the rise of American power in the twentieth century, there was a well-established strain in American political thought that the country had a special destiny. Unencumbered by the corruption and stagnation of the Old World, many thought that the United States would play a special role in the world by offering an inspiring image as a "city on a hill" and the "last, best hope of mankind."

Notably, however, these feelings of national superiority do not particularly translate into a desire among the public to export American ways to other countries, or for the United States to be a superpower wielding hegemonic control over the planet. When American poll respondents were asked to rank a list of foreign policy concerns in 2004, promoting democracy abroad was in eighteenth place, ahead only of improving living standards in poor nations. Pragmatic concerns, such as combating terrorism and weapons of mass destruction and protecting jobs and energy supplies, ranked at the top. Seventy-one percent endorsed focusing on national problems over international concerns, and roughly only one in ten thought the United States should be the world's single leader.

How does this public sentiment relate to the central position of the United States in global affairs? Why, if the American people are not especially eager to build a modern American empire, does the United States play such an overwhelming role in international affairs? Ultimately, the prominence of the United States in world affairs is driven less by any strong desire on the part of its people than by the logic of international relations. Indeed, in its international behavior, the United States is in many ways far from an anomaly. In a competitive, even cutthroat, global environment, countries of all types consistently try to maximize their power with relation to other countries and to seek out whatever political and economic benefits their power can secure for them.

For most of the twentieth century, for instance, China was politically unstable and economically weak, unable to project power commensurate with its size and population. Today, politically unified and economically robust, it is vigorously reasserting itself in Asia and globally. Britain and France, once among the greatest of world powers, continue to maximize their former power by maintaining small nuclear arsenals and holding tight to their veto-bearing permanent memberships on the United Nations Security Council. Recovering from the collapse of the Soviet Union, Russia is using its oil wealth and remaining military strength to reestablish a sphere of influence in neighboring countries. Even Japan and Germany, occupied and humbled after World War II, have begun to move toward a stronger military posture.

And it is not just the so-called "Great Powers" that show a propensity toward expanding their national strength whenever possible. The small European countries of the Netherlands and Belgium became significant colonizers when their economic and military advantages enabled them to conquer less developed peoples in Africa, Asia, and the Americas. These countries may be among the most peaceful and progressive in the world today, but in the seventeenth and eighteenth centuries they proved themselves as capable as any country of practicing repression and committing atrocities. If today their energies are focused on their participation in the European Union, this is probably because membership in the E.U. is likely to be their most effective means for having an impact on world affairs. The former Yugoslav republic of Serbia—about the size and population of Ohio—waged several wars in the 1990s against its neighbors, going so far as to commit genocidal ethnic cleansing in an unsuccessful attempt to become the dominant power in the Balkans. Is there something uniquely aggressive about the Serbs, or are their actions largely explicable in terms of the logic of international relations? History suggests the latter.

Given its unparalleled might, it would thus be quite strange if the United States did not play a major role on the world stage. As discussed in Chapter 1, the American economy and military far outstrip any and all competitors, and the United States has as little hesitation about using its power as other countries do their own. It is true that the United States sometimes claims a special mandate to help to spread democracy, but many of its international actions are designed mostly to advance U.S. national interests. American presidential administrations, Democratic and Republican alike, have consistently supported foreign dictators whom they viewed as allies, especially during the Cold War. And the United States has often declined to intervene militarily in crisis zones, such as Rwanda and Darfur, where there is no oil supply to be secured nor any other compelling strategic interest. Ultimately, such decisions are usually taken on the basis of foreign policy realism and not on behalf of some higher calling in the world—and certainly not on the basis of a strong yearning on the part of the American population to play a dominant role in the world.

Conclusion

Comparative public opinion polls reveal that the United States is quite unusual in its political values and views, although not necessarily the most unusual. Pew researchers have calculated an Exceptionalism Index which shows how different public opinion in some countries is when compared with their neighbors. On this index, the Japanese, with a score of 338, were far more exceptional than Americans, as to a lesser extent were Argentines (240) in South America, Jordanians (236) in the Middle East, or Angolans (235) in Africa. Still, with a score of 220 on this index, Americans stood out among the Western democracies (for instance, France scored 102, Germany 98, and Britain 77). In terms of political views and values, then, Americans are not entirely dissimilar from other developed nations. But on a handful of issues, including religion, the role of government, and national pride, they are quite anomalous indeed.

Further Reading

- *Modernization and Postmodernization: Cultural, Economic, and Political Change in 43 Societies.* Ronald Inglehart. Princeton University Press, Princeton, NJ: 1997.
- *Citizen Politics: Public Opinion and Political Parties in Advanced Industrial Democracies.* Russell J. Dalton. CQ Press, Washington, DC: 2006.

- *America Against the World: How We Are Different and Why We Are Disliked.* Andrew Kohut and Bruce Stokes (of the Pew Global Attitudes Project). Henry Holt and Company, New York: 2006.

Web-Based Exploration Exercise

Visit the Web site of the Pew Global Attitudes Project (<www. pewglobal.com>) and examine the findings of any two polls on a related topic. Compare and contrast views in the United States with those from other countries, looking for common trends and divergences.

Question for Debate and Discussion

We have seen that both political values and the political institutions in the United States are rather anomalous when viewed in comparative perspective. To what extent, and in what ways, do you think that American political values have shaped political institutions, and vice versa?

CONCLUSION
The American Anomaly on Balance

As we have seen throughout this book, it is not very meaningful to speak of the United States as having the world's best or worst political system. Indeed, such judgments are only meaningful when placed into the context of a set of political values to be maximized and needs to be met. Which is to be preferred: Stability over time? Flexibility amid changing circumstances? Responsive politicians? Accountable parties? What is the correct balance between competing values, and how can these best be reconciled? Different individuals will answer these questions differently based on their own political beliefs and personal experiences. Similarly, each country must make these decisions based on its particular circumstances, which are likely to change over time.

Although it may not be possible to generalize about the U.S. political system as being the best or worst in an objective sense, it certainly is possible to identify how different values are maximized or minimized by the particular forms taken by American political institutions and processes. It is also possible to consider how well these dimensions of American politics meet the needs of contemporary life in the United States, and how well they might meet the needs of other countries. This brief conclusion offers some thoughts on how well U.S. politics and government maximize certain key values and what might be learned from the experience of other countries.

Stability

One of the most striking characteristics of U.S. politics and government has been its stability throughout the country's nearly 230 years of history, during which time the country expanded from a cluster of settlements along the eastern seaboard to become a continental power and then a world superpower, mostly under the auspice of the

195

same basic governmental framework. In a world in which tumultuous political change seems to be more the norm than the exception, the U.S. political system has provided an extraordinary degree of political predictability and order.

Consider these anomalous facts: The U.S. Constitution is the first and oldest such continuously functioning document in the world. The same two political parties, and only those two political parties, have alternated in power for the past century and a half. Presidential power has been, without interruption, smoothly transferred for more than 200 years. Elections have been held in the same stable two- and four-year cycles since the founding of the Republic. And once politicians are in office, their terms are fixed, so that governments cannot fall overnight, and except to fill occasional House vacancies, federal elections are never called on short notice. Such executive and legislative stability is in stark contrast to that found in parliamentary systems, enabling longer-range planning and fostering a sense that elected officials have a legitimate right to govern for the duration of their terms. Other than the one great Constitutional failure of the U.S. Civil War, the American political system has successfully managed wars, economic depressions, and social upheavals without there ever having been another revolution, nor a military coup, nor even a dramatic interruption of the regular operation of government. Neither tyranny nor anarchy has managed to undermine American democracy.

Flexibility

While stability is a major goal, however, it can come at the expense of flexibility. The decentralization and dispersal of power in the United States makes it difficult for the political system to adapt to changing circumstances. In order for a new law to come into effect, political actors must come to agreement at nearly two dozen points, with the power to obstruct progress residing with the chairs and memberships of a variety of congressional subcommittees and committees, the leaders and memberships of both the Senate and the House of Representatives, and the president. Then, the participation of state governments, the federal bureaucracy, and the courts may also be needed for the law to be enacted and enforced; yet each of these political actors also has great latitude and even autonomy from Congress and the president. All of these political players have their own political constituencies and agendas, and are often divided along party lines as well, making it a minor miracle that any legislation ever gets passed at all (and explaining why about 90 percent of proposed bills are never enacted into law). Yet if ordinary lawmaking is arduous, it is exponentially harder to change the Constitution itself, with just seventeen amendments having been added since 1791, leaving the U.S. political system with many suboptimal or even outright archaic features. Although the meaning of the Constitution also evolves through new interpretations, this process is often highly contested and usually offers change haltingly at best.

With a limited ability to adapt to changing circumstances, problems can fester for years or even decades under the U.S. political system. Consider that today ethnic and racial socioeconomic disparities remain glaring a half century after the Civil Rights Movement, that millions of people have insufficient or no health insurance in the wealthiest country in the world, and that the United States incarcerates a higher percentage of its population than any other country on the planet. None of these problems is insurmountable, but they persist largely through governmental inertia. By contrast, many parliamentary systems can effect sweeping change at any time. But, of course, those changes can be undone in short order. If the opposition comes into power after an election, it will usually be free to undo the actions of the previous government, contributing to political instability and uncertainty.

Representation

The same fragmentation, decentralization, and dispersal of power that can compromise the efficiency of American government can also promote a high degree of representation. Consider the opposite extreme of the institutional configuration found in the United States, namely, a parliamentary government with a weak upper house in a unitary state with little or no judicial review (such as in Great Britain). Citizens in such countries really have only one major point of access into the political system: their member of parliament, for whom they might cast a ballot as infrequently as every five years. Further, in most parliamentary systems, rank-and-file backbenchers have relatively little ability to influence the work of government, limited mostly to following the lead of their party leaders.

The situation could hardly be more different in the United States, where the average person is represented by at least three elected executives—a mayor, a governor, and a president—and at least six elected legislators—a city or town council member, a member in their state's upper and lower houses, a member of the House of Representatives, and two U.S. Senators. They may also be represented by numerous other local and state officials such as state attorneys general, state comptrollers, county executives, sheriffs, and district attorneys. Given the heavy cost of campaigning and the candidate-centered nature of elections in the United States, each of these elected officials is likely to actively pursue the interests of his or her constituents rather than broader "public good."

If individual elected officials offer a broad variety of opportunities for representation, the U.S. two-party system deprives voters of the chance to choose from the range of political parties that is characteristic of most democratic political systems. In a multiparty democracy, voters are more likely to find a political party with clearly defined positions that fairly closely resemble their own. In systems of four or five parties, the choices are likely to span the ideological spectrum from far right to far left. In systems with eight, ten, or more parties, voters may also be able to find a party that reflects their ethnic, religious, regional, or other interests. In the United States, by comparison, it is much harder for the two major parties to cultivate clear platforms and take sharp positions. Because the Democrats and the Republicans need to capture a majority of the electorate to win, placing a particular emphasis on the so-called swing voters who might be persuaded to support either party. Thus, their policy prescriptions tend to be strikingly similar to one another except on a few key issues, and their views usually hew to the political center.

Those who feel unrepresented by both the Democrats and the Republicans are left with the unpalatable choice of casting a wasted vote for a minor party candidate with virtually no opportunity of winning or voting for the lesser of two evils. Many such individuals may choose to abstain from voting entirely, leaving them and their views completely unrepresented. Thus, it is no coincidence that given frequent, complex balloting that offers few ideological choices, U.S. voting rates are among the lowest in the world. Further, there is a distinct skew in who does and does not vote in the United States: the poorer and less educated, ethnic and racial minorities, and other disproportionately vulnerable populations are the least likely to cast a ballot or to participate in other forms of political activity. Part of this trend can be explained by the various costs of participation, and can be found in other countries as well. But part is attributable to the sense that the two major parties, and the system they control, do not represent the interests of some people enough to motivate them to vote.

Accountability

While the U.S. system promotes a stronger connection between citizens and their individual representatives, it also greatly dilutes the power of political parties. As we have seen, political parties in other countries play a much larger role in the nomination for election and the career advancement of politicians, giving party leaders much greater leverage for enforcing discipline on their elected officials. Similarly, in parliaments, the failure of a party to keep its majority can result in the collapse of a government; in the United States, the consequences are no more dire than a single lost vote on a particular bill. Thus, at election time, voters in parliamentary systems can reasonably consider whether they agree with the priorities articulated by a party and whether those goals have been capably met. In the United States, it far harder for voters to hold parties accountable in this way: the parties do not speak with one voice, and party leaders cannot reasonably be expected to ensure that a particular agenda is carried into action.

Separation of powers and federalism only magnify the problem of accountability. Particularly when the House, the Senate, and/or the presidency are under the control of different parties, it is all too easy for the Democrats to place blame on the Republicans, and vice versa, or for different branches or houses to blame one another. Sometimes, no constructive agenda emerges at all, and the government becomes gridlocked into an inertial pattern; other times, compromise and consensus can lead to the formulation of sensible, centrist public policy. But in neither case can a party claim to have carried out its full agenda. Even when one party wields power at both ends of Pennsylvania Avenue, the institutional separation of Congress and the presidency can prevent the party from fully delivering on its promises. Federalism adds yet another dimension, in which state and federal level officials can blame one another for shortcomings, particularly in the way that federal mandates are carried out at the state level. And finally, politicians can sometimes shift blame to the courts, which regularly employ judicial review to limit the power of legislators and executives. When the time comes for voters to evaluate the performance of their elected officials, it is little surprise that they often are unable to determine who should be held to account.

Conclusion

While there is no perfect political system, some systems can safely be argued to maximize more values for more of their citizens than others. For more than two centuries, the United States has had an unusual combination of political institutions and processes that have rendered it something of an anomaly among the countries of the world. Yet it is a system that in many ways functions well, reflecting an expression of democracy that, while not inherently superior to other political systems, does have some distinctive strengths from which other countries could learn.

Looking forward, sweeping changes to the American political system seem unlikely and would, in any case, probably be undesirable. The deference and respect afforded to established political processes is an enormous value in itself, and sudden or drastic attempts to change them would probably be more damaging than constructive. Still, the challenge of self-government is such that small, slow, incremental, but meaningful ongoing reforms are always necessary. When considering how they can improve upon their political system, Americans would do well to examine their own values and review their own history. But they also should consider the rich insights that the experience of the rest of the world can offer.

FOR FURTHER STUDY:

A Brief Bibliographic Essay on American Exceptionalism

This book is informed by a long history of studies in American exceptionalism, although this literature is not addressed directly in the text. *The American Anomaly* was deliberately written outside of the framework of the exceptionalism debate in order to provide a fresh perspective, as well as to make this volume as useful as possible as a complement to standard American and comparative politics courses. For many students, *The American Anomaly* will ideally mark just the beginning of their study of U.S. politics and government in comparative perspective. For those interested in further pursing this theme, several landmark works in the exceptionalist genre are introduced below, many of which strongly influenced the writing of *The American Anomaly*.

American exceptionalism is generally interpreted to be a school of thought that views U.S. politics and society as a distinctive product of unique circumstances. This school of thought argues that from geographic isolation to social mobility, from the national creed to the immigration experience, the United States has been an exception to usual patterns of historical, social, and institutional development. Although less often used in this way, the word exceptionalism sometimes also carries a connotation of superiority, implying that the United States is an exceptionally outstanding example of democratic practices and thus worthy of emulation abroad. At times in American history, American exceptionalism, under one name or another, has been used to justify territorial expansion within North America, invasion of foreign lands, and assertion of the moral high ground in international relations. On the domestic front, exceptionalism has been expressed by such ideas as the American Dream of upward social mobility and the United States as the "land of opportunity" for immigrants.

Among nineteenth century writers on the theme of American exceptionalism, two stand out. The first is Alexis de Tocqueville, a French nobleman who visited the United States and in 1835 and in 1849 published his often cited two-volume work *Democracy in America*. Based on his travels throughout the young republic, de Tocqueville described a United States that was sharply different from Europe, stressing democracy, liberty, and equality rather than the more traditional hierarchical values of the Old World. Americans, he found, focused heavily on material accumulation, strongly asserted their individual rights, and actively sought to make their own way in the world. Remarkably insightful, even prescient, de Tocqueville remains widely quoted today whenever distinctive patterns of U.S. politics are discussed.

Another outstanding figure of the nineteenth century is the U.S. historian Frederick Jackson Turner. In 1893, Turner published *The Significance of the Frontier in American History*, which placed less emphasis on the country's revolutionary ideals or distinctive social arrangements than on the defining reality of the westward expansion. Turner argued that it was on the ever-shifting frontier—where civilization met and mixed with the untamed—that the American character was forged, becoming more egalitarian and self-reliant, as well as more violent and distrustful of authority. Spawning a massive literature that is both critical and supportive, Turner's work remains a major influence more than a century after it was written.

In 1955, political scientist Louis Hartz published *The Liberal Tradition in America*, which advanced the highly influential argument that American exceptionalism is rooted mostly in a lack of class conflict. In Europe, the political and economic sphere had long been controlled by a wealthy feudal aristocracy, who completely dominated the impoverished masses. As feudalism declined, class conflict ensued, through which the working people cultivated an ideology of socialism and a desire for social welfare programs. In the process, they came to accept high tax rates and a large government administrative apparatus. With no feudal legacy in the United States, and far greater opportunities for individual social mobility, class conflict was relatively muted and neither socialist ideology nor "big government" ever developed. Many of Hartz's arguments about the central role of ideas and culture were validated and expanded by the survey evidence presented in Gabriel Almond and Sidney Verba's *The Civic Culture: Political Attitudes and Democracy in Five Nations* (1965), which compared Italy, France, the U.K., Germany, and Mexico.

One of the giants of the study of American exceptionalism was sociologist Seymour Martin Lipset, who died as this book was being finalized. *The First New Nation: American History and Politics in Comparative Perspective* (1979) examines the social conditions that lead to stable democracy, contrasting the United States with Great Britain, Germany, and France. Lipset's *Continental Divide: The Values and Institutions of the United States and Canada* (1990) explained differences between the United States and its similarly situated neighbor as rooted in the former's revolutionary and the latter's counterrevolutionary histories and ideologies. Lipset also authored *American Exceptionalism: A Double Edged Sword* (1997) and *It Didn't Happen Here: Why Socialism Failed in the United States* (2001, with Gary Marks).

Another giant of the field has been the political scientist Robert Dahl, who is most famous for developing the theory of polyarchy. Polyarchal democracy, Dahl argues, is best understood as a system in which multiple groups and actors interact to produce political outcomes, with no one institution or elite faction having permanent or decisive power. In *A Preface to Democratic Theory* (1956) and *Polyarchy: Participation and Opposition* (1972), he sets out the basic criteria for polyarchal democracy such as competitive elections, freedom of expression, and a broad electoral franchise. Dahl's early work is generally positive about U.S. political institutions and processes, but he becomes more skeptical in later works. In *Democracy and Its Critics* (1989), Dahl argues that no countries can fully achieve democracy. *How Democratic Is the U.S. Constitution?* (2001) analyzes weaknesses and idiosyncrasies of the U.S. Constitutional order, while *On Democracy* (1998) explores the interactions among political institutions and electoral systems. The role of institutions and electoral systems has also been widely examined by the Dutch political scientist Arend Lijphart in such works as *Democracies: Patterns of Majoritarian and Consensus Democracies in Twenty-One Countries* (1984).

Many volumes have been published which analyze the concept of American exceptionalism itself. Charles Lockhart's *The Roots of*

American Exceptionalism: Institutions, Culture, and Policies (2003) analyzes the causes and consequences of American differences in public policy, comparing the United States with Sweden on taxation, Canada on healthcare financing, France on abortion, and Japan on immigration and citizenship. John Kingdon's *America the Unusual* (1999) develops a theory of path dependency to explain how the unique course of U.S. history first created and then reinforced distinctive political institutions and views. Graham K. Wilson takes a more skeptical view in *Only in America?: The Politics of the United States in Comparative Perspective* (1998), arguing that the United States is actually only slightly distinctive. Given their heavily historical and cultural emphasis, all three of these books could serve as a useful complement to the institutional emphasis of *The American Anomaly*.

INDEX